Writing Strands

A COMPLETE WRITING PROGRAM
USING A PROCESS APPROACH
TO WRITING AND COMPOSITION

ASSURING
CONTINUITY AND CONTROL

LEVEL 5

of
a complete writing program
for homeschoolers

a
publication
of

NATIONAL WRITING INSTITUTE
624 W. University #248
Denton, TX 76201-1889

Manufactured in the United States of America

ISBN 1-888344-08-3

For information: Write,   National Writing Institute,
                          624 W. University #248
                          Denton, TX 76201-1889

                          Call,   (800) 688-5375
                          e-mail, info@writingstrands.com

NATIONAL WRITING INSTITUTE PUBLICATIONS

STUDENTS
Writing Strands Level 1
Writing Strands Level 2
Writing Strands Level 3
Writing Strands Level 4
Writing Strands Level 5
Writing Strands Level 6
Writing Strands Level 7
Writing Exposition
Creating Fiction

Communication And Interpersonal Relationships

Dragonslaying Is For Dreamers
Axel Meets The Blue Men
Axel's Challenge

PARENTS/TEACHERS

Evaluating Writing

Reading Strands

Analyzing The Novel:
Dragonslaying Is For Dreamers

INTRODUCTION

This group of exercises in the series called *Writing Strands* is designed to give home-schooled students a grounding in the very complicated process of giving others their thoughts in written form. This level is designed for any student who has completed the exercises in level four of *Writing Strands* or students who, first starting this program, are 15 or 16 years old or, if in public school, would be considered ready for eighth or even up to tenth grade. Of course, fifth and tenth grade students would write much differently, but that is not a problem. Both can experience learning the skills presented in this level. It has been designed to be widely applied, and there are many experiences here that most young writers should have.

Learning to write skillfully is one of the hardest jobs that you have. These exercises will make it easier. Much of the planning and detail of the writing process is presented here.

The writing exercises in this level are in four categories: basic, creation, organization, and description. The exercises in each of these areas will guide you in the development of the skills you'll need.

Rather than increase the work for your parents, this writing process should make it easier for both you and your parents to meet the demands for student writing skill.

When these exercises are completed, you'll have a well-founded introduction to this most difficult skill, and your parents will find it easier to have confidence that this part of the teaching challenge has been met.

For most fifth and up through ninth grade students there are about 90 days of writing instruction in this book. When you finish each writing exercise, if you then spend about a week reading and discussing ideas you get from your reading with your parents, you'll have a language arts program that will last you for a full year. If you're an older student doing some catch up, that's fine, finish sooner.

CONTENTS

HOW TO MAKE

WRITING STRANDS WORK FOR YOU

1. You should have a writing folder containing all of your written work which should be kept for your next level. This will give you a place to store and record your skills, and it's a great thing for your parents to have if they have to make a report on your progress.

2. Both semesters' work have evaluations to be made by your parents. They contain:
   a) The skills you've mastered that semester;
   b) A place for them to comment on your work and a place to list the things you've yet to learn.

3. Each exercise begins with a suggested time for completion. Of course, all students work at different rates. The suggested daily activities can be combined or extended depending on your desire and your parents' goals for your schooling.

4 Many of the exercises suggest that your parents will work with you during your writing period reading what you've written. If this is done, it'll serve two purposes:
   a) It will give you constant feedback and will allow your parents to catch many writing problems before they appear in your final papers.
   b) It will greatly cut down on your parents' correcting time. Most of the paper reading can be done during your writing sessions, so, even though you'll be writing much more than you previously have been, your parents should be able to help you more using even less of their time.

5. At the end of each semester's work there's an evaluation form where you or your parents can list any continuing problems you have:
   a) The form at the end of the first semester should contain a listing of the problems that you should work on during the second semester.
   b) The year's-end evaluation form should list the problems that you can solve next year.

PRINCIPLES

The following principles were adopted by National Writing Institute before work began on *Writing Strands*. They were our guides in the initial stages of the design of the exercises.

1. Every person needs to learn to express ideas and feelings in writing.

2. There is no one right way to write anything.

3. The ability to write is not an expression of a body of knowledge that can be learned like a list of vocabulary words.

4. Parents and their students both learn in any effective writing situation.

5. The product of each student's writing efforts must be seen as a success for at least the following reasons:
   a) A student in a writing situation is not in competition with anyone else.
   b) There is no perfect model against which any effort can be compared for evaluation, so there is no best way for any student to write.
   c) Every controlled writing experience will help a student improve in his or her ability to express ideas.

6. All student writing efforts are worthy of praise. The most help any parent can give at any point is to show, in a positive way, what is good about a piece and how it might be improved.

7. Any writing lesson assigned, which is done independently by the student and does not have a parent's constant feedback in the form of reinforcement and suggestions, represents a missed opportunity for the student.

8. All writing at any level is hard work, and every writer should be encouraged to feel the pride of authorship.

9. All authors need to be published. This can be accomplished by having their work read to other family members, posted on bulletin boards (refrigerators), printed in "books" or read by family members.

10. Students should be encouraged to find that writing is exciting, rewarding and fun.

LEVEL FIVE

EXERCISES * SKILLS * OBJECTIVES

Exercise 1: **Narrative Voice Attitude**
Skill Area: Basic

1. Understanding that narrative voices have attitudes
2. Identifying narrative voice attitudes
3. Creating attitudes in narrative voices

Exercise 2: **Interesting Sentences**
Skill Area: Creation

1. Adding detail to sentences
2. Eliminating patterns in sentence structure

Exercise 3: **Arguments That Win**
Skill Area: Organization

1. Recognizing a valid argument
2. Recognizing the points of an argument
3. Writing an effective argument

Exercise 4: **Omniscient and Limited Knowledge**
Skill Area: Creation

1. Understanding that narrative voices can have different degrees of knowledge
2. Identifying degrees of knowledge
3. Creating different degrees of knowledge for narrative voices

Exercise 5: **Write for Action**
Skill Area: Basic

1. Understanding that the passive voice is not exciting
2. Understanding that the active voice is exciting
3. Writing in the active voice

Exercise 6: **Narrative Voice Position**
Skill Area: Description

1. Understanding that authors have to place their narrative voices in positions
2. Being able to place a narrative voice in a position

Exercise 7: **Where to Start**
Skill Area: Organization

1. Understanding that there are many ways to organize a group of items
2. Understanding that organizing methods have value
3. Organizing items for description

Exercise 8: **Dialogue**
Skill Area: Basic

1. Punctuating dialogue
2. Recognizing speech patterns and copying them
3. Identifying who is speaking by the way the dialogue is written
4. Working with others

Exercise 9: **An Author Makes the Reader Feel**
Skill Area: Creation

1. Understanding that a reader's feelings are controlled
2. Understanding that these feelings help the reader understand the story
3. Understanding some techniques authors use
4. Using reader-control techniques

Exercise 10: **Out of Time**
Skill Area: Basic

1. Writing dialogue that follows the story line
2. Changing tenses in dialogue
3. Controlling the use of tenses

Exercise 11: **My Thumb**
Skill Area: Description

1. Seeing an object as a group of parts
2. Organizing what is seen
3. Organizing descriptive writing

Exercise 12: **Flashback**
Skill Area: Organization

1. Understanding what a flashback is
2. Knowing how flashbacks work
3. Using flashbacks in writing

Exercise 13: **Foreshadowing**
Skill Area: Organization

1. Understanding foreshadowing
2. Knowing how foreshadowing is used
3. Using foreshadowing in writing

Exercise 14: **New House**
Skill Area: Creation

1. Controlling what the reader understands
2. Describing an object so that the reader will see it in his mind

Exercise 15: **The Balloon**
Skill Area: Creation

1. Understanding that characters have emotions
2. Creating characters who are motivated by their emotions
3. Writing a story which has complicated characters

Exercise 16: **Writing Letters**
Skill Area: Organization

1. Understanding the principles of writing business letters
2. Learning where to place the parts of business letters
3. Writing business letters

STRANDS

Two of the most desired characteristics of any writing program are for it to allow for continuity of instruction from grade to grade and to allow for control of the learning process by the teacher.

Below are the strands, the exercises that present the strands and where they're found in this text.

NOT RULES,

MORE LIKE SUGGESTIONS

In almost everything we do, there are rules (like laws), and then there are what we call "rules." The rules that are like laws are written and we all accept these as the rules we have to live by. Then there are the "rules," the things that we *should* do, that we agree to do, and things that make life nicer for everyone if we do them.

This is also true in writing. As an example of the difference in the rules of writing, look at the rule (law) that says that every sentence must start with a capital letter. This is written down and we all must write using this rule. A "rule" of writing is that we use an exclamation point only once a year.

The following "rules" are just strong suggestions. You can violate them if you want to. It might be good to keep in mind however, that if you do, your readers will look at your writing the same way that the company at dinner might look at you if you burped at the end of the meal. So, below is a short list of the "rules" of writing:

1. Don't use exclamation points! This makes any writing look amateurish and fuzzy. If you're saying something that's important, the way you say it should be strong enough so that you don't have to tell your reader that it's important by using exclamation points at the end of your sentences.

2. Don't underline the titles of your papers. The only time there should be an underline in one of your titles is when you use the names of books or magazines.

3. Skip a line after the title in any paper you're giving to someone else to read.

4. Never write *The End* at the end of anything you write for a schooling exercise.

5. Don't try writing humor until you've studied it and really know the difference between being funny and being corny. (Those places in this book where I've tried to be funny and was corny will give you an example of what I mean.)

6. Don't skip a line between paragraphs.

7. Always leave a margin at the bottom of each page.

8. Check your papers for clichés before you write the final drafts.

STUFF I LEARNED LAST YEAR ABOUT WRITING
THAT I FEEL REALLY GOOD ABOUT

1. _____

_____

2. _____

_____

3. _____

_____

4. _____

_____

5. _____

_____

6. _____

_____

7. _____

_____

8. _____

_____

#1 NARRATIVE VOICE ATTITUDE

Skill: BASIC

It may take you six days to learn that:
1. The narrative voices in fiction have attitudes
2. You can identify narrative voice attitudes
3. You can create attitudes in your narrative voices

PREWRITING

Days One and Two:

When we read fiction, we're not reading what the author thinks and feels. We have no way of knowing what they are. The only contact we have with the author is through the narrative voice. This is the voice the author's invented to talk to us through the marks on the page.

Sometimes this voice is made to care about what happens to the characters in the story, and sometimes this voice doesn't care at all. These two voice situations are called **subjective voice** and **objective voice**. Every writer must understand how these two voices work and the effect the choices have on readers.

SUBJECTIVE VOICE:

This is the attitude the narrative voice has when the author wants to let the reader know that his *voice has feelings* for what is happening to his characters. This voice lets the reader know this by the comments it makes. (This will make sense in a moment.)

If we were to write about a baby mouse which has been caught by a cat and we were to want to have our narrative voice be **subjective** (care), we would have to have our narrative voice indicate how it feels by the comments it makes and the words it chooses to use. We could write it the way it is written on the next page:

In the following passage, I have made bold the words used that indicate that the narrative voice is **subjective.** (That it cares what happens to the mouse.)

> **The poor**, *exhausted mouse was now too tired to move. It was not badly hurt and could live, but each time it tried to escape, the* **awful** *cat would reach out and put a paw on it. It was* **pathetic** *to see the mouse try again and again but be caught just as it thought it could get away.*

Our reader will know this is subjective because of our choice of words. We have chosen to have our voice **feel sorry** for the baby mouse, and we have let our voice's feelings be known by calling the mouse *poor*, by calling the cat *awful,* and by saying that it was *pathetic* to watch what was happening. (The narrative voice has these feelings.)

OBJECTIVE VOICE:

This is the attitude the narrative voice has when the author does *not want* the reader to know what it feels about what's happening to the characters. This voice *hides* what it feels.

If we were to write about the same mouse, but with an **objective** narrative voice, we would have our narrative voice tell our reader what happens, but we wouldn't let the reader know that the voice feels one way or the other about the event (It **does not care.**). If we were to want our voice to be **objective**, we could write about the mouse being caught this way:

> *The exhausted mouse was now too tired to move. It wasn't badly hurt and could live, but, each time it tried to escape, the cat would reach out and put a paw on it. The mouse tried again and again but was caught just as it thought it could get away.*

You'll recognize here that the voice doesn't let the reader have any idea about how it feels about either the cat or the mouse being in this situation.

The author decides to make his voice **subjective** or **objective** based on how the author wants to create feelings in the reader. An author chooses whether to have a subjective or objective voice for two reasons:

1. The author creates a closer bond with readers by showing that both of them feel the same way about what's happening.

   In our subjective voice example with the mouse, we want the reader to feel sorry for the mouse. We have almost said to the reader, "We both feel that same way about that poor mouse."

2. The author wants to control what the reader feels about what's happening in the story, but the author doesn't want to tell the reader how to feel. There might be a good reason for us to want our reader not to feel sorry for the mouse. Maybe we

2

want our reader to be glad that the mouse has been caught.

Let's see how we could control our reader's feelings by rewriting that piece. In this example we might want our reader to feel sorry for a very poor woman who has been overrun with mice. In fact, there could be so many mice about her small farm that they might be eating all of her grain. She could be alone and have no one to help her, and if the mice were not controlled, she would not have enough grain to feed her chickens in the winter, and both they and she would starve. We could show our reader the old woman trying to block the holes the mice had eaten in her grain house. We could have her lie in bed at night and imagine she hears her small stock of grain being eaten, knowing that there would be no way she could get any more in the long winter just ahead.

We could have her find a starving kitten along the roadside. She could take it home and share her small supply of food with it. Our reader would begin to feel sorry for our old woman, would like the kitten and would grow to hate the mice which were sure to eat so much that the woman and her animals would starve.

We could watch her take the kitten to the barn with her when she goes to feed her chickens. Our reader could see the mice scatter at her approach. The old woman could cry out at seeing how much of her grain they had already eaten. She could see the new holes the mice had cut in the sacks. Our reader could see that soon there would not be any grain left at all.

Now we can rewrite the piece about the cat and the mouse and control our readers by making them feel good about the cat catching the mouse:

You may want to work with your parent and together decide where the voice is **objective**, but now the readers' are led to be glad the kitten has caught the mouse.

> *The old woman put her kitten on the barn floor and placed her hands on both sides of her face as she cried out, "Soon there won't be any left at all."*
> *She began to examine the grain sacks, and she found where new holes had been chewed in many of them. Her chickens would surely starve, and then she would starve. What was she to do, she thought, when the snow piled around her house and barn and she would not be able to leave her property for months?*
> *She looked for her new kitten as she realized that it might also starve in the winter. She saw the kitten had caught a small mouse!. The exhausted mouse was too tired to move. It was not badly hurt and could live, but each time it tried to escape, the cat would reach out and put a paw on it.*
> *Her new kitten could save them all.*

In this example we have reversed how we want our reader to feel, so now our reader will like it that the cat has caught the mouse. Authors might choose to use an objective voice because they want their readers to create their own feelings about what's happening in their stories. Sometimes readers get more involved in what's happening when they feel that the authors aren't trying to control their feelings.

WRITING

Day Three:

You'll write in a **subjective** and then in an **objective** way about the same incident.

For today, we'll work together on this first exercise. We'll create a narrative voice which will want our reader to feel sorry for a rabbit which has been caught in a trap. I'll start you off and then you complete the paragraph.

> *There had been an unusual amount of snow. It was sad to see the small rabbit having such a terrible time digging down deep enough to get to any of the dried grasses and the small limbs of the bushes it had to eat that winter. The trap snapped shut.*

Your reader should feel sorry for the rabbit after reading your finish to the paragraph. (Be sure to include the narrative voice's feelings about what's happening.)

For this next paragraph you're writing today, you're to write about the same rabbit, but this time you're to take out any **subjective** feelings used in the first version. It is to be an **objective narrative voice** which tells the reader about the rabbit getting caught by the trap.

Day Four:

You'll write about the same rabbit getting caught. This time you'll have to shift your reader's sympathy to a man who has put out the trap to catch the rabbit.

You'll have to talk about why the man wants the rabbit caught in the same way we talked about the old woman who had the cat which caught the mouse. But, you'll still have to create a narrative voice which is **objective**.

4

Your writing will *end* with this sentence: (This is not just to make it harder.)

> *The small rabbit was having a hard time digging down deep enough to get to any of the dried grasses and the small limbs of the bushes it had to eat. The trap snapped shut.*

Days Five and Six:

You'll invent your own narrative voice attitude. You'll invent your own situation. You'll decide how you want your reader to feel and you'll write to create that feeling in your reader. This isn't easy to do. I'm asking you to do something that takes lots of practice to do well. So, if you don't feel too good about what you write for this lesson, that's okay. Keep working on this idea and the skills will come to you.

Write at the top of the first page: **1**) what **narrative voice attitude** you've selected and **2**) how you want your reader to **feel**.

Your paper should have your **name, first and last**, in the upper right corner and below that the date. Skip two spaces and write your **title.** Skip one line and identify the **attitude** for your narrative voice and how you want your reader to **feel**. Skip one line and **begin** your narrative.

The **top** of your paper should look like this:

```
                                              (Your Name)
                                              (The date)

 (Skip two spaces)


__(First line)_____#1  NARRATIVE VOICE ATTITUDE_____
__(Skip one line)_____
__1.  Narrative voice attitude:_____
__2.  Reader should feel:_____
 (Skip one line)
_____
 (Your narrative starts here)
_____
~~~~~~~~~~~~~~~~~~~~~~~~~~~~~~~~~~~~~~~~~~~~~~~~~~~~~~~~~~~~~

    (Even margins all sides and page numbers bottom center except page #1.)
```

I recommend you take the next week off from writing..

PROGRESS REPORT

Name:_____ Date:_____

Exercise # 1 NARRATIVE VOICE ATTITUDE

Copy your best sentence for the week on the lines below.

_____

_____

Name one mistake you made this week that you can fix and will avoid next week.

_____

_____

Write the sentence that had this mistake in it.

_____

_____

Write the sentence again showing how you fixed this mistake.

_____

_____

Comments:

#2 INTERESTING SENTENCES

Skill: CREATION

It may take you three days to learn to make your writing more interesting by:
1. Adding detail to sentences
2. Eliminating patterns in sentence structure

PREWRITING

Days One and Two:

As a creative writer, you have two jobs. The first is to give your reader information. The second is to entertain your reader, or at least make your writing interesting. (This's the hard part.)

This exercise is designed to give you practice in making what you write more interesting than it would be if you were to use it just to pass on information.

The following sentence is all that is needed to pass on the information that a very old man was mad:

The old man was mad. (That's straight information and not very interesting.)

If we were to want to make that sentence more interesting, we'd have to add to that basic piece of information. There would have to be descriptions that would let our reader see the mad old man, understand why he was mad and make us feel some way about him being mad. Watch what happens to that sentence when we add detail about how the old man acts when he's mad:

The old man was so mad he couldn't speak; he just jumped up and down in one spot. (A more interesting old man, right? But still not too gripping.)

Watch what happens when we add detail about why the old man was mad:

When the old man woke up and found his bridge was gone, he was so mad he couldn't speak; he just jumped up and down in one spot. (Better?)

7

We have given our reader an idea about how the old man feels about his bridge being gone and how he acts. Now see what happens when we add detail about why he feels so strongly about his bridge:

The old man was homeless and lived under the bridge and called it his home, so, when he woke up and found his bridge gone, he was so mad he couldn't speak; he just jumped up and down in one spot. (Now that we know why he was so mad, his reaction to his bridge being gone is much more interesting.)

Let's add one more bit of information to this sentence. Let's add who's watching him and see what that does:

Bill watched the old man who lived under the bridge wake up and find his home gone, which had made the old man so mad he couldn't speak; he just jumped up and down in one spot. (We have added another person reacting to the old man's anger. Much better, right?)

WRITING

(If you don't write in this book, you can give it to your younger brother or sister to use. Use the outlines to guide you and use your own paper. If your parents want you to write here, fine. Always do as they suggest.)

Now it's your turn. Here's just basic information in sentence form.

The old man lost his bridge.

Your job is to give your reader this information but in a way that makes it interesting.

Add the reason the old man lost his bridge.

_____

_____

_____

Add the length of time the old man had to be without his bridge.

_____

_____

8

_____

Now write a short sentence that gives your reader nothing but basic information. Then write it two more times on another page and add new details to it each time. When trying to think about what interesting details to add, try **how, why, when**, and **where**.

1._____

_____

_____

2._____

_____

You've found you can write a sentence that's interesting. Now you can learn how to write a number of sentences and not have them sound alike.

Young writers sometimes create patterns with their sentences by starting them all in the same way. Listen to how this sounds:

> *Bill saw the old man standing in the stream. Bill asked him why he was standing there. The old man said he was looking for his bridge. Bill thought this was strange. He asked the old man, "How did you lose your bridge?"*
>
> *The old man answered, "When I went to sleep it was over me, and when I woke up it was gone."*
>
> *Bill looked closely but could not see anything that looked like part of a bridge.*

All of these sentences begin with a **subject** which is followed immediately by a **verb**. This is pretty boring reading, even when the subject's interesting. Read the sentences again, but see how much better they sound when the subject-verb pattern is broken:

> *When he looked toward the stream, Bill saw the old man standing in the water. Bill asked him why he was standing there. The old man, looking up and down the stream, said that he was looking for his bridge. Bill thought this was strange. "How did you lose your bridge?" he asked.*
>
> *"When I went to sleep," the old man answered, "it was over me, and when I woke up it was gone."*
>
> *Even when he looked closely, Bill could not see anything that looked like part of a bridge.*

9

You can see that the subject-verb pattern of the sentence structuring in the second version of that passage has been broken. This gives the writing variety. You can do this as easily as any author. All you have to do is look at what you have written and change the structuring of your sentences.

Here's another example of how variety can be put into sentences structures. Notice that each of the following sentences contains the same information. It's the structuring of the sentences that's different.

1. *Bill saw a field of blue flowers, and in the center of this large area there was an old bridge.*

2. *In the center of a large field of blue flowers, Bill saw an old bridge.*

3. *In front of Bill an old bridge rose over a large field of blue flowers.*

4. *Blue flowers covered the large field in front of Bill, and in the very center was an old bridge.*

5. *An old bridge rose from the large field of blue flowers that lay before Bill.*

You're to write, on another sheet of paper, the sentence below five different ways. Change the structure of the sentence each time.

> *Bill walked back to the stream to tell the old man that he might have found his bridge for him.*

Day Three:

You'll have a chance to combine the skills you practiced on days one and two. You learned to add detail to your sentences and then to put variety into their structuring. I'll give you a group of sentences and your job will be to make them interesting by adding detail and to make the reading of them interesting by restructuring them. For the first part, think of **how, why, when**, and **where**. For the second part, break the **subject-verb pattern.**

1. *Bill found the old man by the stream.*

2. *Bill told the old man that he might know where his bridge was.*

3. *The old man said he would give Bill anything to get the bridge back.*

4. *Bill thought this would be a good way to get the old man to eat a good dinner.*

5. *The old man agreed to eat a good dinner if Bill got his bridge back for him.*

PROGRESS REPORT

Name:_____ Date:_____

Exercise # 2 **INTERESTING SENTENCES**

Copy your best sentence for the week on the lines below.

_____

_____

Name one mistake you made this week that you can fix and will avoid next week.

_____

_____

Write the sentence that had this mistake in it.

_____

_____

Write the sentence again showing how you fixed this mistake.

_____

_____

Comments:

#3 ARGUMENTS THAT WIN

Skill: ORGANIZATION

It should take you five days to learn to:
1. Recognize the points of an argument
2. Recognize a valid argument
3. Write an effective argument

PREWRITING

Day One:

Until now you may have thought an argument sounded something like this:

> *"Did too."*
> *"Did not."*
> *"Did so."*
> *"No, it didn't."*
> *"Oh, yeah?"*
> *"Yeah!"*

This is what some children sound like when they can't think of anything to say to support what they feel or want.

What educated people call an argument is when people who don't agree with other people present their ideas in organized ways.

When educated adults present arguments, each argument has four parts:

1. A **statement**
2. An **explanation** of any parts of the statement the other person might not understand
3. **Support** for the position of the statement
4. A **conclusion**

1. **THE STATEMENT** is what you believe to be true or what you want. This can sound like the statements on the next page:

That was a foul ball.
I saw the dime first.
I should be able to stay over at Janet's house.
I should not have to do the dishes again tonight.

The **statement** should be a short, easy-to-understand sentence. Your reader will never agree with you if it's not perfectly clear what you're arguing for. So, your argument should start with a short, clear statement.

2. **THE EXPLANATION** should explain the parts of your statement that might not be clear, or, if you're not sure your reader would understand them, they should be explained. This can sound like one of these explanations:

> *I mean that I want to go over to Janet's house after dinner and stay with her all night and come home tomorrow before noon.*

There's no need to write the explanation part of the argument if you're sure the statement is clear and easy to understand.

3. **THE SUPPORT** wins the argument. In most cases an argument is won by the person who has the best presentation of facts, not by the person who shouts the loudest or talks the most.

When you're in an argument with other people and they begin to raise their voices, you know that they've run out of things to support their side of the argument. At this point you know you've won.

You must support your argument with facts, reasoning and quotations from authorities. You're not an authority. It doesn't support your argument to say *Because* or *I think so* or *I'm older*. You must support your argument with real support. It could sound like this:

> *Dr. Spock says that young girls sometimes need to get away from their parents for a night.*

> *Janet's mother has invited me, and she said she'll call you if you'd like to talk to her.*

> *The health teacher told us that young people need to begin to be independent and this is good if they have supervision.*

> *Janet's mother and father will be there all evening and all night.*

> *I'll call you before I go to bed to let you know I'm okay.*

13

Our minister said last week that young people need to practice having close friends outside of the family circle.

Janet's father said that he'll pick me up after we eat supper and will drop me off tomorrow before noon.

You let Billy and Alice stay with their friends when they were no older than I am, and that must have been good for them, because look at how well they turned out.

4. **THE CONCLUSION** asks your reader to agree with you. An argument is really an attempt to sell someone an idea. You must ask your reader to buy what you want to sell. In the above example, the girl wants to sell her mother the idea that she should be allowed to stay the night at Janet's house.

A conclusion for this argument might read like this:

So, I would like you and Dad to discuss this and then consider giving me permission to stay at Janet's house tonight.

WRITING

Day Two:

Today you'll outline an argument. You should have your statement written, any explanation that's necessary and a list of the ideas you'll use as support.

Days Three and Four:

Write the supports for your statement. You're not an authority. You should quote other people. Use reasoning and facts. What is called personal anecdotal evidence is no good. An example of this is*: Smoking can't be that bad, Uncle Harry has smoked for 80 years.* Begging has no place in an argument. The following would not work as support in the example:

Can I stay at Janet's house? Huh? Please, Huh? Huh? Please, Mom, Can I? Pretty Please.

You should write the conclusion today.

Days Five and Six:

The argument you wrote for day two was to your parents or another adult. Today you'll write the opposite side of it. The argument you write for them should be constructed the same way yours was, but it should be about why you should not get what you want or be able to do what you want to do. (Why not take a week off from writing?)

PROGRESS REPORT

Name:_____ Date:_____

Exercise # 3 **ARGUMENTS THAT WIN**

Copy your best sentence for the week on the lines below.

_____

_____

Name one mistake you made this week that you can fix and will avoid next week.

_____

_____

Write the sentence that had this mistake in it.

_____

_____

Write the sentence again showing how you fixed this mistake.

_____

_____

Comments:

#4 OMNISCIENT AND LIMITED KNOWLEDGE

Skill: CREATION

It may take you four days to learn that:
1. The narrative voices in fiction can have different degrees of knowledge about actions and characters
2. You can identify degrees of knowledge
3. You can create different degrees of knowledge for your narrative voices

PREWRITING

Day One:

The narrative voices with which authors talk to their readers can have different degrees of knowledge: **omniscient** or **limited**.

1. **OMNISCIENT**:
This is the telling of everything all characters know and do.

2. **LIMITED**:
This is the telling of some of what characters know and do. There are two choices.

A. If a narrative voice **is a character** in a story, the voice would be **limited** to what **that character could know**.

B. If a narrative voice **is not a character** in a story, and the author doesn't wish the narrative voice to tell the reader some things, the **author can limit** what **information** is told to the reader.

1) **OMNISCIENT**:

Authors never select a totally omniscient narrative voice. There's always some limiting. Otherwise, authors could never get stories told, because they would have to tell their readers what each character, even dogs and goldfish, are thinking and doing at all times. Usually, authors use a limited omniscient narrative voice, and the thoughts of just one or two of the characters are given.

This limited omniscient voice is almost never a character in the story. It doesn't make sense that a person in the story would know what other characters are thinking.

If we were to write a story with **a limited omniscient narrative voice**, we would have to tell our reader what our characters are thinking.

If we were to write about a boy and his father with such a voice, we might want to get into both of their minds and tell what they both are thinking.

There might be other characters in the story, but we wouldn't *have* to tell our reader what they're thinking. It could sound like this:

> *Bill's father turned the old station wagon into the drive. It was blocked by Bill's bike. His father thought, "Oh, no, not again. How many times have I told that boy not to leave his bike in the drive? I don't know what I've got to do to that kid to get him to have some responsibility."*
> *Bill was in his room putting a new tape in his stereo. He was standing by his desk when he saw the blue car turn into the drive and stop short because of his bike. Bill dashed down the stairs and through the dining room to the kitchen. As he was easing the screen door closed, he thought, "By the time Dad gets into the house I can have the mower going in the back yard. It was dumb of me to leave my bike in the drive. Now, what can I say was the reason I did that?"*

2) LIMITED TO WHAT A CHARACTER COULD KNOW:

Let's write about the same boy and his father in the same situation. But let's have our voice's knowledge limited to what a character could know.

A **limited narrative voice** for our story can be either:

1. A **character** in the story
2. A **non-character**

CHARACTER

If we were to have our narrative voice be a character, but not be part of the **immediate action,** and be **limited in knowledge** to what that character would be able to see and hear, it might read like the example on the next page:

I could hear John turn in the drive, but there was a squeak of brakes. Glancing out the window, I saw that Billy had left his bike in the drive again. What a way to start the evening. I heard Billy pounding down the stairs, and I remembered his father had told him to mow the lawn. By the time John came into the kitchen through the side door, I could hear the mower start in the back yard. I wondered what Billy would have to say about leaving his bike in the drive.

The narrative voice in the above passage is the mother, but she isn't part of the action and has a limited knowledge of the events because she can't get into the heads of the other characters, and she's upstairs and can't see much of the action.

NON CHARACTER

If we were to have our narrative voice be a **non-character,** but **limited in knowledge**, it might sound like this:

Billy's father turned the old station wagon into the drive. It was blocked again by his son's bike. He had told Billy many times not to block the drive.
When he stepped out of the car, his eyes swept across the lawn. The grass had not been cut. He had told Billy to be sure and cut the lawn today. By the time he reached the side door he smiled, for he must have heard the lawn mower in the back yard.

In this case, the narrative voice doesn't tell about Billy running down stairs to start the lawn mower, or about the mother looking out the window. The voice can see the father smile but can't *know for sure* that it's because of the sound of the mower.

After you've read through the above explanation, your parent may want to go over parts of it with you. If there are things that aren't clear, be *sure* to ask questions, because you'll have to work with this later today and for the next two days.

If you can identify the degrees of knowledge in the following passages, you understand enough to be able to control the knowledge of your own narrative voices.

1. Narrative voice knowledge:_____

Bill stopped at the door to the gym. Mr. Rains saw him standing there and wondered what his problem was. Bill had been acting strange lately, and his coach was really worried about him.

18

The other players also had noticed a change in Bill. They had been keeping an eye on him for the last month or so. Bill hadn't realized that they were worried about him, but he'd seen them looking at him a lot lately, and wondered what their problem was.

2. Narrative voice knowledge:_____

Bill walked into the gym. He usually went directly to the parallel bars, but on this day, he didn't even look at the coach or at the other boys; he just walked on to his place and began to practice. The coach looked away for a moment, then again looked at Bill, who was bent down over his shoe. He frowned as he continued to stare at Bill.

3. Narrative voice knowledge:_____

Wow, I thought I was going to be late and was the last one in the door. I had just hit the gym when Bill came to the doorway and stood there. He looked like he wasn't gonna come in.

The coach gave him one of his famous looks and sorta smiled. Bill then came in and went clear to the back of the room, where he bent over his shoe like there was something wrong with it.

WRITING

Days Two through Four:

In the next three days you're to write three pieces, but longer than the three short samples above, one for each of the narrative voices you've studied. Any narrative subject will work.

You should have narrative voices with:

1. **Limited omniscient knowledge**
2. **Knowledge limited to what a character could know**
3. **Knowledge limited to what the author wants his reader to find out** in ways other than by hearing the characters think

Set your paper up to be like this example page:

(You'll have at least three pages, one for each narrative or degree of knowledge.)

(Your Name)

(The date)

(Skip two spaces)

#4 OMNISCIENT AND LIMITED KNOWLEDGE

(Skip one line)

First narrative: Limited omniscient knowledge

Second narrative: Knowledge limited to what a character could know

Third narrative: Knowledge limited to what the author wants his reader to learn other than by dialogue

(Even margins all sides of paper and page numbers bottom center)

(There's a lot here. If you don't understand it all now, read through the exercise again and talk about it with your parent. If it still doesn't make sense, don't worry, it will soon.)

The answers to the three questions about degrees of knowledge are: 1. omniscient, 2. limited, and 3. limited to what a character would know.

I recommend you take a week off from writing.

PROGRESS REPORT

Name:_____ Date:_____

Exercise # 4 **OMNISCIENT AND LIMITED KNOWLEDGE**

Copy your best sentence for the week on the lines below.

_____

_____

Name one mistake you made this week that you can fix and will avoid next week.

_____

_____

Write the sentence that had this mistake in it.

_____

_____

Write the sentence again showing how you fixed this mistake.

_____

_____

Comments:

#5 WRITE FOR ACTION

Skill: BASIC

It may take you four days to learn:
1. Passive voice is not exciting to read
2. Active voice can be exciting to read
3. Some ways to make your writing more exciting to read

PREWRITING

Days One and Two:
Some of the stories that students write are exciting to read and some are dull. One thing you can do to make your writing more exciting to read is to write in the active voice.

ACTIVE VOICE:

The active voice has the subject of the sentence doing the action. It sounds like this: *John caught the mouse*. Of course, *John* is the subject, and John did the catching.

PASSIVE VOICE:

The passive voice has the subject of the sentence acted upon. It sounds like this: *The mouse was caught by John*. In this case, *mouse* is the subject, and the mouse was caught by something else, *John*.

(All you have to do is identify the subject of your sentence and be sure that subject does something and doesn't have something done to it.)

WRITING

I've written **about half** of a very short story for little children that has a lot of passive voice in it. Your job will be to recognize the sentences that are written in the passive voice. As you do this, think of the effect the writing has on the reader.

22

The ravine was the home of the large black snake. All of the animals which lived in the neighborhood of the ravine were afraid of the long, silent killer. When the snake—who was called the Black One by the small animals—was out of its hole hunting, the mice, rabbits and ground birds were very quiet.

This spring there were nine eggs that had been hatched and small black snakes had been produced. These small killers were loved by The Black One. Live food had to be found by each of the baby snakes, for they could not be fed by the mother snake.

They could not be shown how to glide silently through the tall grass or how to lie still and let the baby rabbits play near them until they were close enough to be bitten and wrapped in tight coils.

It was very dangerous for all of the small creatures who lived in the wooded ravine. The babies were warned by their parents about the killers. But what the parents said didn't seem important to them.

After a large number of the babies who lived in the ravine had been eaten, all the parents were called to gather at the edge of the woods. A decision had to be made about what to do about The Black One and her young.

When there had been much discussion by the parents of the small animals, it was decided to hire a raccoon to come and kill the black snakes.

But, there was a problem. What would a raccoon want for pay? Clover was offered by the rabbits. Nuts were offered by the squirrels. Worms were offered by the moles. Seeds were offered by the mice. Of course, none of the offerings was right for payment to a raccoon.

A suggestion was made by a mother quail. "Why don't we ask the raccoon what he'll want to be paid to work for us? Then what he wants can be gathered by us to pay him."

This was thought to be a good idea by the other animals. The plan was agreed upon by everyone. The raccoon would be invited to come and meet with the animals.

The day of the meeting came and all of the parents of the small animals were met by the raccoon in the shade of the meeting tree.* In the center of the clearing there was a large stump. On this sat the raccoon. All around him were the worried parents. He was asked by them what he would want to kill the snakes.
He said, ". . . .

Days Three and Four:

You're to write the rest of this story in active voice. Remember that stories have:

1. Time and place   3. A Problem   5. A Resolution
2. Characters   4. A Climax

(As an example, I've changed one passive voice sentence for you.)

* *In the shade of the meeting tree, on the day of the meeting, the raccoon met all of the parents of the small animals.*

23

PROGRESS REPORT

Name:_____ Date:_____

Exercise # 5 WRITE FOR ACTION

Copy your best active voice sentence for the week on the lines below. (Check)

_____

_____

Name one mistake you made this week that you can fix and will avoid next week.

_____

_____

Write the sentence that had this mistake in it.

_____

_____

Write the sentence again showing how you fixed this mistake.

_____

_____

Comments:

#6 NARRATIVE VOICE POSITION

Skill: DESCRIPTION

It may take you three days to learn that:
1. Authors have **choices** about where they'll place their narrative **voices**
2. You have the same choices all authors have   (*See why unintended rhyme is bad?*)

PREWRITING

Day One:

An author has two choices of position for his narrative voice. These choices are somewhat like the choices an author has for character knowledge that you studied in exercise four.

If the **voice is a character** in a story, that character has to be somewhere. This means that the character who is **the voice is limited** in what could be seen and heard from that position. The voice must tell the story from what that character knows by being in that position. Of course, this character can move around in the story, so this character/voice will be able to tell the story from each position in the story the character occupies.

The other narrative voice position choice an author has is one of having the **voice be a non-character**. In this case **the voice is not limited** to being where a real person would be. This voice can be high above the ground looking down and seeing lots of different actions at the same time. This makes it possible to have an omniscient voice.

Or, the author could choose to have his **non-character voice limited,** as if the voice were a real person.

So, an author has these two choices for the position of his narrative voice:

1. If his **voice is a character** in the story, the voice position is **limited** to where a real person might be.

2. If his **voice is a non-character** in the story, the author has two more choices:

25

A. The voice can be **anywhere** and **see all things**
B. The voice can be **limited** to being where a real person might be

Here's an example of choice number one—the **voice is a character** in the story (in this case a student—one of Bill's friends):

The Voice is moving into the front room of a home.

> *As soon as I walked into the room I knew that something was up. All the family members were sitting still and no one was talking. This was strange. I figured Bill somehow was behind whatever was going on. I was a little late getting home for dinner, but not so late that everyone should be just sitting there.*

Here's two examples of choices of number two **(a non-character)**. This first example has the voice as a **non-character who is *not limited*** to being where a person might be.

The Voice is **Everywhere**:

> *Bill was just rounding the corner at **First and Oak Street**. The twins and Mr. Smith were sitting in the **living room**, Mr. Smith in the big chair and the twins on the couch. Mrs. Smith was in the **kitchen** putting the roast back in the oven. All of Bill's friends were in the **basement** waiting for Bill to come home.*

Notice that this voice can see and understand what's going on in more than one place at a time. This voice knows what's going on where Bill is, the living room and the basement all at the same time.

This second example is of a narrative voice which is a **non-character** but one which is **limited to being in one position** in the same way a person/character would be.

The Voice is **in the living room**:

> *Mr. Smith turned to the twins and said, "Where in the world is your brother? The kids in the basement must be getting impatient by now." He rose from his chair and stepped into the kitchen and said, "Dear, do you think Bill forgot that we asked him to come right home after work?"*

Notice that, because this voice is limited in position and is in the living room when Mr. Smith talks to the twins and then follows him into the kitchen when he talks with his wife, it cannot know what is going on in the basement with the kids waiting for the surprise party for Bill or where Bill is, and so cannot tell this to the reader.

WRITING

You're to write **three pieces of narration**. Write one piece for **each of the choices** an author has for the position of his narrative voice:

1. With the **voice as a character** (which will make his position **limited** to where a person could be)

   With the **voice as a non-character**:

2. **A. Not limited** in position (can be **anywhere** or **everywhere**)

3. **B. Limited** in position (as a character would be **limited**)

Today you'll write the first piece. It doesn't have to be a story. It can be just an event. Anything. You should have a number of people in it. One of the **characters will be the narrative voice**. It would be easiest if this **limited** voice were to speak in first person. This means using the word *I*. After you've written a rough draft, make sure your parent reads your paper.

Day Two:

Write the same piece of narration but use a narrative voice which will be a **non-character**, which will **not be limited** in position. Your voice will be able to tell of the action which takes place in more than one location at the same time.

Day Three:

This time the **non-character** narrative voice **will be limited** in position in the same way a narrative voice who is a character would be limited.

Set your **final** paper up this way:

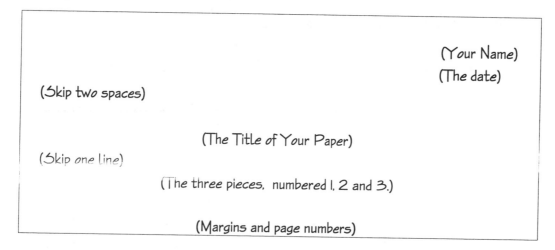

27

PROGRESS REPORT

Name:_____ Date:_____

Exercise # 6 NARRATIVE VOICE POSITION

Copy your best paragraph for the week on the lines below. (Read that sentence again.)

_____

_____

_____

_____

Name one mistake you made this week that you can fix and will avoid next week.

_____

Write the sentence that had this mistake in it.

_____

_____

Write the sentence again showing how you fixed this mistake.

_____

_____

Comments:

#7 WHERE TO START

Skill: ORGANIZATION

It may take you six days to learn that:
1. There are many ways to organize objects
2. Organizing has value
3. You can organize objects for descriptive writing

PREWRITING

Day One:

One of the jobs authors have is to make what they're writing easy to understand. If an author were to write about a number of objects, it would help the readers if the objects in the description were presented to the readers in a logical way.

There are lots of ways to do this. Some work better for some things than others do.

How a logical method of presentation might aid a reader can be seen if we were to describe a coffee can full of marbles.

If we were to describe the marbles as we take them out of the can, our reader would soon get mixed up. It might read like this:

> *In this can there are 200 marbles. The first one out of the can is a blue cat's eye. It is one-half of an inch in diameter. Its color is dark blue with some lighter specks. The color is in the middle of the marble. The second marble is clear with no color. It is three-quarters of an inch in diameter. The third marble is a solid pale-green color. It is smaller than the first two. The next marble is another cat's eye, but this time the color is brown.*

It's easy to see that, after taking two hundred marbles out of the can, the reader would soon be as mixed up as the marbles.

See what a difference it makes when I impose some order on the description:

29

In this can of 200 marbles there are 50 cat's eyes. Of these there are 25 which are blue and 25 which are brown. There are 100 marbles of clear glass. There are 50 of a solid color. Of these, there are 25 blue, 15 green and 10 brown.

All the cat's eyes are one-half of an inch in diameter. Of the clear glass marbles, 50 are one-half of an inch in diameter, and the others are three-fourths of an inch in diameter. All the solid-colored marbles also are three-fourths of an inch in diameter.

WRITING

You'll write a paper describing a large group of objects which are similar but not identical. Some possibilities are:

1. Buttons
2. Spools of thread
3. Toy soldiers
4. Crayons
5. Spoons
6. Nails

The steps in the organization of your objects could include:
1. Categorizing
2. Counting
3. Ordering (deciding which you'll describe first)
4. Sub-categorizing—making categories of the sub-groups (*Of the clear glass marbles, 50 are one-half of an inch in diameter. . . .*)

The easiest way for you to categorize the objects is to examine them for major characteristics. These characteristics could include:

1. Color
2. Size
3. Shape
4. Cost
5. Importance
6. Weight
7. Texture
8. Perforations
9. Use

There will be other characteristics that you'll think of that'll work just as well for your choice of objects.

Day Two:

On day one you decided on the ordering of your objects' characteristics. Today you'll write the **introduction** to your paper.

You'll have to think of a reason why you decided to describe your objects. One reason that you could use is that you were bored one day when you were sick and decided to look at a box of buttons. You found the buttons all mixed together and decided to organize them and put them in envelopes which you would label by color, size and shape. This could read like this:

> *One day last week while I was sick, I decided to organize a button box. I was amazed to find so many buttons in one place. Someone must have been saving them for years. Now I knew where all the buttons from my shirts had gone. My parent said it would be nice if I were to separate all the buttons that were alike and put them in envelopes and then label the envelopes. What a job. The first thing I had to do was categorize the buttons. I decided to use color, size, shape and number of holes as the categories.* (Sorry, you can't use buttons now)

Make sure your parent reads your work when you're finished.

Preparation:

Rewrite your **introduction** and have your parent look at it at the start of this session.

Days Three and Four:

Write the **body** of your paper. Make sure there's enough detail that your reader can "see" what you're talking about.

Preparation:

Rewrite your **body**.

Day Five:

For your **conclusion**, you could say something like this: *When your mother told your father what you had done, he was so pleased with the results that he asked you to do the same thing with the big box of nails and screws in the garage.* (Not this either)

Day Six:

Write the final copy in ink but be sure and check spelling and punctuation.

For this paper only, you should label the parts of your paper. Indicate where the **introduction**, the **body** and the **conclusion** begin. This is so your parent can be sure you understand the structure of this paper.

(Your Name)
(The date)

(Title of Paper)
(It could be: "#7 Where to Start")

Introduction

Body

Conclusion

(Even margins all around. Page numbers on all pages except #1)

I recommend you take the next week off from writing.

PROGRESS REPORT

Name:_____ Date:_____

Exercise # 7 **WHERE TO START**

Copy your best sentence for the week on the lines below. (That wasn't a trick.)

_____

_____

Name one mistake you made this week that you can fix and will avoid next week.

_____

_____

Write the sentence that had this mistake in it.

_____

_____

Write the sentence again showing how you fixed this mistake.

_____

_____

Comments:

#8 DIALOGUE

Skill: BASIC

It should take you six days to learn how to:
1. Punctuate dialogue
2. Recognize speech patterns and copy them
3. Make it clear who is talking by the way you have your characters speak
4. Work with your parent to produce a piece of writing that will make both of you proud

PREWRITING

Day One:

In books written for young children, who is speaking is made clear by the endings on sentences that sound like: *he said* or *Janet said*.

In stories written for children who are just a little older, the identifying labels are sometimes put into the middle of the characters' speeches, like this: *"Hand me that hammer," Bill said to his friend, as he picked up some of the very small boards that he was using to make his sister's doll house, "and I'll show you how easy this is."*

An even more sophisticated way to write is to sometimes skip the speaker identification label, like this:

Bill's mother, Mrs. Jones, looked at the smashed doll house and climbed to Bill's room and asked him, "What in the world could have done that to Janet's doll house?"
"What happened to Janet's doll house?"
"Come and look at it."
"What did she do to it, Mom?"
"Janet said she thought you may have sat on it."
"Who, me? Why would I do a dumb thing like that?"
"Did you?"
"Did I what?"
"Did you do what Janet said?"
"What exactly did she say again?"

34

You may not have realized it, but much of that conversation didn't have identifying labels attached to the speakers. Go back and look for them. (*Do it.*)

In this exercise you'll write a piece of dialogue and not label the speaker every time.

Day One:

You and your parent might work together today. You could agree on a story you both could read. It should be one in which there's lots of obvious conflict and dialogue. You both should read this story before day two.

Day Two:

Pick a scene in the story that has two characters. It will be easier for you if you pick ones who are the ages of you and your parent. You should study the way these two characters talk in the rest of the story. You'll be writing dialogue like the author did for these characters.

List your character's speaking characteristics:

Name:_____Age:_____ Sex:_____

How Smart: Bright:_____ Average:_____ Dumb:_____

Uses words which are: Long:_____ Short:_____ Familiar:_____ Strange:____

Speaks formally:_____ Uses slang:_____ Speaks: Quickly:_____ Slowly:____

Is respectful of others:_____ Is a smart aleck:_____

Likes to talk:_____ Does not like to talk:_____

WRITING

Day Three:

You and your parent might now do the preparation for the writing of a bit of dialogue for the story. This means that you'll pick the point in the story where you can add to the dialogue of the two characters interacting, or where they're talking together about something. It's at this point that you'll add the dialogue you'll soon write.

Your writing should have at least 15 speaking times for each character. It should sound like the two characters in the story are talking about some event in the story. It should sound like it's a part of the story written by the author.

Day Four:

You both will write just one side of this dialogue. Today it will help if you talk through

35

the event (have a conversation about this event) as if you were the characters in the story. One of you can pretend to be one character and the other can pretend to be the other character.

Before you start this exercise, check over your list of speaking characteristics for your character. In your practice you'll want to use those characteristics.

Day Five:

You can write the dialogue you and your parent practiced on day three. Look at any story, novel or at the short piece of dialogue in this exercise to see how to punctuate your writing.

(Three rules that will help:)

1. Each new speaker gets a new paragraph.
2. All punctuation marks go inside the quotation marks.
3. Separate what a character says from the rest of the sentence by commas.

Day Six:

Today you and your parent can read your conversation to the rest of the family. It will be like a play in that you each will read the part you wrote.

You should start reading in the story about one-half of a page before you come to the part you added to the story. It should sound to the rest of the family members as if what you wrote was written by the author.

You should read at least a paragraph of the story after you have finished reading the piece of dialogue you wrote. If your family doesn't follow along with you in the book, it might be fun to see if they can tell what was written by the author and what was written you and your parent.

I recommend you take the next week off from writing.

PROGRESS REPORT

Name:_____ Date:_____

Exercise # 8 **DIALOGUE**

Copy your best sentence for the week on the lines below.

_____

_____

Name one mistake you made this week that you can fix and will avoid next week.

_____

_____

Write the sentence that had this mistake in it.

_____

_____

Write the sentence again showing how you fixed this mistake.

_____

_____

Comments:

SPELLING LIST

Every time you or someone else finds a misspelled word in your papers, write it in the column below. This is not to give you a list of words to study; rather, it's a listing to let you know what your problems are. I'd suggest you pick one word that gives you trouble each week. One that you use a lot. Learn that word this week, and next week pick another word to learn. Watch for that word in all of your reading and writing. In this way, in two or there years, you'll have a good basic spelling vocabulary.

(Check the *Evaluating Writing* manual for this process.)

_____

_____

_____

_____

_____

_____

_____

_____

_____

_____

_____

_____

_____

FIRST SEMESTER REPORT

WRITING SKILLS MASTERY

FIFTH LEVEL WRITING EXERCISES

Student:_____ Date:_____

Parent/Teacher:_____

Skill   Needs
Mastered Experience

Exercise 1: Narrative Voice Attitude
Skill Area: Basic

_____   _____ 1. Understanding that narrative voices have attitudes
_____   _____ 2. Identifying narrative voice attitudes
_____   _____ 3. Creating attitudes in narrative voices

Exercise 2: Interesting Sentences
Skill Area: Creation

_____   _____ 1. Adding detail to sentences
_____   _____ 2. Eliminating patterns in sentence structure

Exercise 3: Arguments That Win
Skill Area: Organization

_____   _____ 1. Recognizing a valid argument
_____   _____ 2. Recognizing the points of an argument
_____   _____ 3. Writing an effective argument

Exercise 4: Omniscient and Limited Knowledge
Skill Area: Creation

_____   _____ 1. Understanding that narrative voices can have different degrees of knowledge
_____   _____ 2. Identifying degrees of knowledge
_____   _____ 3. Creating different degrees of knowledge for narrative voices

Exercise 5: Write for Action
Skill Area: Basic

_____ _____ 1. Understanding that the passive voice is not exciting
_____ _____ 2. Understanding that the active voice is exciting
_____ _____ 3. Writing in the active voice

Exercise 6: Narrative Voice Position
Skill Area: Description

_____ _____1. Understanding that authors have to place their narrative voices in positions
_____ _____2. Being able to place a narrative voice in a position

Exercise 7: Where to Start
Skill Area: Organization

_____ _____ 1. Understanding that there are many ways to organize a group of items
_____ _____ 2. Understanding that organizing methods have value
_____ _____ 3. Organizing items for description

Exercise 8: Dialogue
Skill Area: Basic

_____ _____ 1. Punctuating dialogue
_____ _____ 2. Recognizing speech patterns and copying them
_____ _____ 3. Identifying who is speaking by the way the dialogue is written
_____ _____ 4. Working with other students

#9 AN AUTHOR MAKES THE READER FEEL

Skill: CREATION

It may take you five days to learn that:
1. An author controls the feelings of his reader
2. Feelings help a reader understand what the author is saying
3. There are techniques authors use to control feelings
4. You can use these techniques in your writing to create feelings in your reader

PREWRITING

Day One:

The better you get at reading, the more detail there will be in what you read. Young readers read mostly for action and conflict. Older people, like your parents, read for an understanding of what the characters are feeling and for descriptions of people and places.

In this exercise you'll write to give your reader feelings about the "places" in a story. Sometimes this is called *mood*.

You'll need some examples of how this is done. When writers write, they can describe anything they want to and can ignore what they don't want their readers to know. What they do is focus their readers' eyes on what they want them to see. It's almost as if they were holding the readers' heads, pointing them at certain things—much as we might hold a dog's head when we want the dog to see a squirrel in the yard.

What the writer describes for the reader then must be important to the writer, and so it must be important to the story.

It may help you to see what I mean if you understand what is important to the story in the following descriptions. Your parent may want to point out what I want the reader to see by what things I've chosen to describe and how I've described them.

> *Bill sat with his back against the large and rough oak tree and looked at the maples in the ravine below him, which had turned golden in the morning sunlight.*

41

He had been there for just a short time when he saw a slight movement in the top of one of the taller trees. There was a rough chucking sound, and he could see a gray tail flip each time the squirrel called. The big male ran along the slender branch and jumped in the clear light of the morning sun to another tree closer to the hill. That branch swayed with the weight, then shot upward as the squirrel jumped again.

Bill lost track of the squirrel for a short time but soon saw it again on the ground, scuffling in the yellow leaves. The squirrel must have found what it had been looking for because it ran straight up the trunk of an old stump and sat on its top eating a nut it was holding with both paws.

In this example, I want the reader to focus on the squirrel, which is certainly of interest to the character, Bill. It must be that I want the reader to understand something about Bill's interest in the squirrel. He could be a naturalist or a hunter. He might be a nature photographer or a lover of animals.

I rewrote that piece to focus the reader's attention on something else. I used the same character, Bill. I put him in the same place—on the hill looking down on the ravine. I could even have put in the squirrel if I had wanted to. But, this time, the reader will be led to concentrate on something else.

Bill sat with his back against the large and rough oak tree and looked at the maples in the ravine below him, which had turned golden in the morning sunlight.

He had been there since before dawn. When he had first sat down, the ravine had been black, and he could see nothing below him. He had been able to make out the dark outline of the large trees on the eastern side of the woods, for their shapes stood out against the lighter sky.

Gradually his world lightened, and then. . .the tips of the trees on the hill caught the morning sun. It was as if their tops had burst into flame.

Their leaves shone brightly and sparkled with dew in the sunlight, but still the ravine was dark. He was able to watch the light fall down the trees as the sun rose, giving the trees life in color from the tops down. When the sun finally hit the bottom of the ravine, Bill was surrounded with golden light. It seemed to him as if he were inside some giant yellow crystal, and his world glowed and shimmered in the clean, new day.

In this second version of the same scene, the reader is made to focus on other details. This gives the reader different feelings about the story. Now Bill might see the squirrel, but that is not the point of him being there. The narrative voice wants the reader to enjoy the beauty of the color in the morning. This then must be the point of the description.

WRITING

Days Two and Three:

You'll now have a chance to try this focusing of your readers on what you want them to "see." Your first description will focus your readers' attention on the happy things in some building in your area or town. You could use a restaurant, library, fire station, town hall, or any other public place. You'll make your readers feel good about this place. You might include:

1. Bright colors
2. Posters
3. Bulletin boards
4. Large windows
5. Colorful books
6. The quick movements of busy people

As soon as you've done as well as you can, ask your parent to read your work and make suggestions.

Days Four and Five:

You're to describe the same place again, only this time you're to make your readers see it as a place which is not good and happy. You might write about:

1. The dirt on the windows
2. The cement walls
3. The dirty floors
5. The evidence that the people who are there are bored or at least not happy in their work
6. The dull voices
7. The sounds of people moving in their work
8. The smells

(Think about this idea:)

When you give something to another person to read, you're saying to that person, "Here's my best thinking on this subject." Or, you could be saying, "Look at what a good creative writer I am. I've just created this. Read it."

If what you hand to that person has obvious mistakes in it (things you could have avoided), you're saying, "I don't really care what you think so I didn't try very hard to do a good job with this piece of writing."

Set up the final copy of your paper like the example on the next page.

43

(Skip two spaces)

_____ # 9 AN AUTHOR MAKES THE READER FEEL _____

(Skip one line)

First *place* narrative: Reader Likes

_____

_____

_____

_____

_____

_____

_____

_____

Second *place* narrative: Reader Does Not Like

_____

_____

_____

_____

_____

_____

_____

_____

(Watch margins and page numbers)

I recommend you take the next week off from writing.

PROGRESS REPORT

Name:_____ Date:_____

Exercise # 9 AN AUTHOR MAKES THE READER FEEL

Copy your best paragraph for the week on the lines below. (*See, here it is again.*)

_____

_____

_____

_____

Name one mistake you made this week that you can fix and will avoid next week

_____

Write the sentence that had this mistake in it.

_____

_____

Write the sentence again showing how you fixed this mistake.

_____

_____

Comments:

#10 OUT OF TIME

Skill: BASIC

It may take you three days to learn you can be good at:
1. Writing dialogue
2. Changing tenses in dialogue
3. Controlling your use of tenses

PREWRITING

Days One through Three:

I've in my mind a comedic bit which involves an old man who has a great deal of trouble with time. He gets mixed up in his skit when he tries to tell someone from another time zone what time it is. This is what happens:

He's at an airport that has been built in two time zones (the time zone marker runs right through the building). A boy, who must be in a great hurry for he keeps looking at his watch, comes up to him and asks him what time it is.

The boy must be very anxious about the time for he paces back and forth. Each time the comedian looks at his watch and tells the boy the time, the boy has moved. When he moves, he crosses the time zone and time for him changes. The comedian can't keep track of what time zone the boy's in.

Right away things start to go wrong for the comedian. When he says that it's three o'clock, the boy moves two feet closer to him, and the comedian then says "No, it's two o'clock." When the boy hears this he steps back and looks at the comedian, who says, "Now it's three o'clock."

It's when he tries to explain the time difference to the boy that things really get confusing. As he's talking, he explains that he'll use past tense in explaining why it had been two o'clock when he was on one side on the time-zone line, and then use present tense in explaining why it was three o'clock on the other side of the line.

When he starts to tell the boy what time it will be when he gets home, he tries to use future tense and he gets both of them all messed up.

WRITING

Using the above description as a scenario, You're to write this conversation that this comedian might have with a young person. Keep in mind:

1. **Each new speaker should have a new paragraph.**
2. **Commas and periods should be inside the quotation marks in each sentence.**
3. **There should be a comma between what a character says and what that character does.**

Here's an example of the use of these rules:

The comedian pulled his watch out of his pocket, and, taking one step to the side, said, "I am seeing on this watch that it is three o'clock here, but it will be two o'clock there," and he pointed to the floor near his feet.

The boy looked up at the old man and asked, "Why?"

"Because, when I moved from here to there, time changed to three o'clock, and now I'm in the future by one hour," he said, and he shook his head as he took a step to the right.

This was hard for the boy to understand. He had thought the old man was confused, and he said, "But I thought you just said it was two o'clock."

The old man got angry. He began to talk very loudly when he said, "Of course. That is exactly right. It will be two o'clock, but now it is three o'clock and it was two o'clock over there. And when the 2:35 flight gets me home, it will be half past one, because it is a two hour flight, and I will have lost two hours and be in the past by I don't know any more," and he threw up his arms and stepped into two o'clock.

Your parent may want to point out where the comedian is having trouble.

In your paper, you should indicate in parentheses which tense the old man is using each time he speaks. It should look like this:

The old man asked, "What time is it over there?" **(present)**

The boy held out his arm, showing the old man his watch, and said, "Here it is three o'clock, Sir."

"I will be there in three o'clock when I take one step to the left," the old man said. **(future)**

"I don't understand how that works," the boy said.

"Where I left from, it was two o'clock there, **(past)** *but for you, when you get there, it will be three o'clock here,* **(future)** *but it will be three o'clock there* **(future)** *when it was two o'clock over there,"* **(past)** *he said, pointing at the floor."*

It might help you if you and your parent were to draw a line across the living room floor with a piece of string. Set up time zones on different sides of the string. Find two watches or clocks and set them for the different time zones. Then when you're ready to write your dialogue, you can play the parts of the people in the airport in the different time zones. If you don't do something like this, it could get confusing.

You could ask your parent or your brother or sister to help you by playing the part of one of the characters. If you don't have a number of clocks you could draw clock faces on paper with the different times on them.

You may go on with this conversation, or you may start a new one for this exercise. Each day ask your parent to check your work.

Your narrative voice will be speaking in past tense for the whole dialogue. It will be the old man who will change tenses. The boy *may* change tenses when he asks questions such as: *"It will be two thirty over there?"* That question is in future tense. The same kind of change with the following in present tense: *"Why is it one thirty over here?"*

(What time is it in the airport lobby?)

2:30 Eastern time zone

(Time Zone Line) **AIRPORT**
                  LOBBY

1:30 Central time zone

(I guess the time always depends on where you are.)

I suggest that you take the next week off from writing.

PROGRESS REPORT

Name:_____ Date:_____

Exercise # **10 OUT OF TIME**

Copy your best sentence for the week on the lines below.

_____

_____

Name one mistake you made this week that you can fix and will avoid next week.

_____

_____

Write the sentence that had this mistake in it.

_____

_____

Write the sentence again showing how you fixed this mistake.

_____

_____

Comments:

#11 MY THUMB

Skill: DESCRIPTION

It might take you nine days to learn to:
1. See an object as a group of parts
2. Organize what you see
3. Describe in an organized way what you see

PREWRITING

Days One and Two:

Your parent may let you use a plant for this exercise and you can place it in front of you. You'll study it. You must learn to see. You think you know how to do this, but observing is a skill that has to be learned. This is something artists must learn to do. I feel that learning to see is one of the most important activities there is.

What you'll know about the world will depend on how well you learn to observe and organize in your mind what you've seen.

Your first job, when given the task of describing something, is to understand what it is you're to describe. This means that you have to look closely and critically at the object. You'll have to know what is there. You must decide what all of its parts are and what they look like.

For this exercise, I'll list for you what's there. Soon you'll have the job of describing an object, and I'll not be there to help you decide what its parts are.

Remember, when you describe things, you start with major areas first, then go on to describing the details. You should use the same process in this description. You'll need a ruler.

On the desk are:
1. A pot
2. Potting soil
3. A plant

We'll start with the pot. The things you can tell about the pot by looking at it are:

1. How big it is
2. What it's made of
3. What color it is
4. What shape it has
5. How many pieces there are
6. How it's decorated
7. If it has any holes and how many there are (look at the bottom)
8. What the relationships of its size, color and shape are to the plant

We'll start with number 1. How big it is. There are lots of ways to measure a pot:
A. How tall it is
B. What its diameter is at the top
C. What its diameter is at the base
D. If it has a rim at the top, how wide the rim is
E. How big the hole(s) in the bottom is(are)
F. If the pot has a base to hold water, how tall the base is
G. How big around and how thick it is
(There's more.)

So far we've just looked at the pot, and we have nine areas we've seen. In just one of those nine areas, size, we have seven different measurements to make.

If each of the other eight areas of the pot have as many measurements to them, we'll have 56 sentences we can write just about the pot, and we haven't even looked at the soil or the plant yet. You now understand what I meant when I said that the skill was in the looking.

If you were to do this same kind of looking at the whole object (the plant, soil and the pot) you'd end up with pages and pages of description. You could be working on this exercise until next June and still not be done. (Great way to spend a spring.)

We'll have to make this exercise shorter than that. What you're to do is make a list of what you see and not try to describe what you see. This then will be an exercise in looking and organizing but not one in describing.

You're to do for the soil and the plant what I did for the pot. Make lists of what you see. Don't describe what you see, just list what you're looking at.
The parts of the soil you're to list are:
1. Color
2. Thickness
3. Texture
4. Position in the pot, and anything else you can see.

51

You'll list the parts of the plant—like the stem(s), the leaves and the flowers (if any)—and the ways of describing them.

WRITING

Days Three and Four:
Now that you've had an exercise in seeing, you'll describe your thumb. Today and tomorrow you'll list the areas of observation (what you see).

Think of things like:
1. Color(s)
2. Shape(s)
3. Size(s)
4. Movement(s)
5. Texture(s)
7. Materials it's made of: skin, nail, hair, (dirt?)

Days Five through Seven:
You'll be examining, measuring and describing your thumb. Follow your outline.

Day Eight:
You don't have a complete paper on your thumb yet. You need an introduction, which should contain the following information:

1. **How old your thumb is**
2. **Whether it's a boy thumb or a girl thumb.** (If you don't know how to tell this, ask your parent.)
3. **What kind of thumb it is. It could be a soft, gentle thumb that likes to stay clean and do the dishes, or it could be a strong thumb that likes to play ball and work on bikes or cars.**

Day Nine:
You still don't have a complete paper yet. You need a conclusion, which should contain the following information:

1. **How you feel about your thumb**
2. **Why you feel this way about it**
3. **How your feelings have changed about your thumb since you've studied it so closely.**

You should organize your paper the way this example page is organized.

(Your Name, first and last)
(The date)

(Skip two spaces)

#11 My Thumb

(Skip one line)   (Skip *no* other lines)
INTRODUCTION:
   1. Your thumb's age
   2. Whether it's a boy thumb or a girl thumb.
   3. What kind of thumb it is.
BODY:
   1. Color(s)   (Do *not* label the parts of your paper, like BODY)
   2. Shape(s)
   3. Size(s)
   4. Movement(s)
   5. Texture(s)
   7. Materials it's made of
   8. Any other things you can think of   (Attitude?)
CONCLUSION
   1. How you feel about your thumb
   2. Why you feel this way about it
   3. How your feelings have changed about your thumb

(Even margins all sides   (Page numbers bottom center
of every page)   except for page #1)

I recommend you take the next week off from writing.

PROGRESS REPORT

Name:_____ Date:_____

Exercise # 11 **MY THUMB**

Copy your best sentence for the week on the lines below.

_____

_____

Name one mistake you made this week that you can fix and will avoid next week.

_____

_____

Write the sentence that had this mistake in it.

_____

_____

Write the sentence again showing how you fixed this mistake.

_____

_____

Comments:

#12 FLASHBACK

Skill: ORGANIZATION

It may take you three days to learn:
1. What a flashback is
2. How flashbacks work
3. How to use flashbacks in your writing

PREWRITING

Days One and Two:

Sometimes writers use flashbacks when they want to start their stories with an exciting event and then go on and show what caused it. Other times they're used when writers want to give their readers some general background information—like what kind of a childhood a character had.

A flashback is just what it sounds like—a flash back to some prior time. This is done on TV, and we know it's happening when we hear the dream music and the picture goes fuzzy around the edges.

It's just as easy in reading to recognize when writers use flashbacks. They tell the readers that they're doing this by using paragraph breaks and the past perfect tense (which has the word *had* in it) two or three times. It looks like this:

> *Bill carried the small plastic bag of mud in his pocket. He knew just where he was going to put it.*

(Here comes the flashback: Notice the use of the past perfect tense, *had*.)

> *Having collected some dirt last night, **he had mixed** just enough water with it to make it firm and slightly gooey. One of his sandwich bags from his lunch **had been perfect** to put it in. He had patted it out and trimmed it until it looked just like a brownie.*

Now we end the flashback by going out of the past perfect tense and back to the story line in a new paragraph:

Bill waited until everyone was watching the game. He knew where Janet had put her sack lunch. Checking the kids at the picnic one last time, he hurried to Janet's lunch bag.

I wanted to show my reader where Bill had found the mud and how he had kept it. I also wanted to start my narrative with Bill thinking about using the mud for a special purpose. I was able to solve this problem by using a flashback.

WRITING

Write a short narrative and use a flashback. Remember, when you want to shift into a previous time, you have to use the past perfect tense. This means your first two or three verbs will have to have the word *had* with them. When you want to get back out of the flashback situation, take up the story at the same place you left off to go into the character's past actions. (Your narrative should be about three pages long.)

This list may help you to understand the order of the steps in a flashback:

1. You're using **past tense** in a narrative.
2. You want to **interrupt the story to show** your readers something that has happened **before the time you're telling about**.
3. You must use a **flashback.**
4. You introduce your readers to this prior time by using the **past perfect tense two or three times**, then you can **use past tense for the rest** of the flashback.
5. You tell your readers what you want them to know in the **flashback section.**
6. You **change out** of the flashback by a **paragraph change**, and you **pick up the story line** again where you left it.
7. You **go back to** using **past tense.**

Day Three:

Today you should give your parent your paper. Your parent should be able to mark (*) your paper where the flashback begins and ends.

Write an explanation to your parent telling how flashbacks work and what you did to write your story section that contained a flashback. Use the outline on the next page to organize this explanation.

(This chart may help you organize your explanation of how flashbacks work)

(Your Name, first and last)
(The date)

(Skip two spaces)

#12 Flashback

(Skip one line)

How Flashbacks Work and What I Did:

(Skip one line)

1. I was in past tense in a narrative.   (Skip _no_ other lines)
2. I introduced a flashback to before the time I was telling about.
3. I began the flashback by a paragraph change, and
4. I used the past perfect tense two or three times.
5. I used past tense for the rest of the flashback.
6. I wrote the flashback section.
7. I changed out of the flashback by a paragraph change.
8. I picked up the story line where I left it.
9. I continued narrative using the original tense.

(This is just an outline. You should use full sentences in paragraphs.)

(Even margins all sides   (Page numbers bottom center
of every page)   except for page #1)

I recommend you take the next week off from writing.

PROGRESS REPORT

Name:_____ Date:_____

Exercise # 12 **FLASHBACK**

Copy your best sentence for the week on the lines below.

_____

_____

Name one mistake you made this week that you can fix and will avoid next week.

_____

_____

Write the sentence that had this mistake in it.

_____

_____

Write the sentence again showing how you fixed this mistake.

_____

_____

Comments:

#13 FORESHADOWING

Skill: ORGANIZATION

It may take you three days to learn:
1. What foreshadowing is
2. How foreshadowing is used
3. That you can use foreshadowing in your writing

PREWRITING

Days One and Two:

When authors want to hint that something might happen to characters in their stories, they sometimes employ a device called foreshadowing. This is just what it sounds like—a hint of what's to come. It's like a shadow going before a man when the sun is behind his back.

One of the times foreshadowing is used is when authors want to create feelings of suspense. They can indicate to readers that there might be danger for characters by hinting that the danger's in places the characters might soon find themselves.

As an example of how this works, I'll give you the start of a story scenario:

> *Janet asks her father if she can go with her friend to the beach. Her father says that this is fine with him, but that she will have to fill the right front tire on the car, because it has a slow leak and he doesn't want her to get stuck with a flat. (At this point the reader has been given a hint that at some time in the story Janet and her friend will have a flat tire).*

WRITING

You'll write the start of a short story in which you'll use foreshadowing.

You'll have to think of something that might happen to one of your characters. Then you'll have to give your reader a hint that the thing will happen to that character. You can invent your own or use one of the following scenarios:

1. Two boys want to go camping in the woods. A convicted murderer has just escaped from a nearby prison.

2. Janet wants to go for a walk with her friend, but her father warns her that a thunderstorm is predicted.

3. Mr. and Mrs. Jones have been married for 10 years. Mrs. Jones has been wondering if her husband remembers the anniversary date is near. When she's picking up the newspapers in the den, she notices that the travel section is on the top of the pile.

4. Mrs. Jenkins has just told the group of kids that she has this unnatural fear of snakes. Bill collects snakes.

5. The homeschool support group is planning on taking a charter bus on a field trip to the museum. Bill's pair of pet mice have been having lots of babies, and he's been wondering what to do with all of them.

If you follow this outline it may help you foreshadow an event.

1. Create your characters.
2. Give them an activity in which they want to engage.
3. Introduce your reader to something that, if the characters get involved in it, it could be interesting for them.
4. Head your characters toward that time or the place where the event might occur.

Day Three:

Today you'll have a chance to check your paper for spelling and punctuation errors. When this is done, give your paper to a family member and have that person tell you what might happen to your characters if your foreshadowed event occurs.

Make sure your parent reads your rough draft before you start to write the final copy.

Preparation:

Check for spelling and punctuation and give your parent the final copy on day four.

Again, write a paper explaining how something works, in this case, foreshadowing. Use the outline on the next page to organize your paper.

(Your Name, first and last)

(The date)

(Skip two spaces)

#13 Foreshadowing

(Skip one line)

How Foreshadowing Works and What I Did:

(Skip one line)   (Skip _no_ other lines)

1. I wrote a piece of narration in which I used foreshadowing, and
2. Created my characters
3. Gave them an activity in which they wanted to engage
4. Introduced my reader to something that, if the characters get involved in it, it could be interesting for them
5. Headed my characters toward that time or the place where the event might occur

(This is just an outline. You should use full sentences in paragraphs.)

(Even margins all sides
of every page)

(Page numbers bottom center
except for page #1)

I recommend you take the next week off from writing.

PROGRESS REPORT

Name:_____ Date:_____

Exercise # 13 **FORESHADOWING**

Copy your best sentence for the week on the lines below.

_____

_____

Name one mistake you made this week that you can fix and will avoid next week.

_____

_____

Write the sentence that had this mistake in it.

_____

_____

Write the sentence again showing how you fixed this mistake.

_____

_____

Comments:

#14 THE NEW HOUSE

Skill: DESCRIPTION

It may take you four days to learn that you can:
1. Control what your reader understands
2. Describe an object so that your reader will "see" it in his mind

PREWRITING

Days One and Two:

When authors describe objects, they have in mind what they want their readers to understand, and so they control what and how their readers "see." They can write about any of thousands of characteristics. But they select what they describe so as to give their readers the information they want them to have.

This is a two-part exercise. Both parts will take you two days to complete. Try to write at least **four** pages for each part.

WRITING

In this paper you'll describe a large house. The house is new but you'll not tell your reader this. **But, this is what you'll want your reader to understand.** The way you describe the house will give your reader this knowledge. You can describe the:

1. Lawn
2. Shrubs and flowers
3. Sidewalk
4. Paint on the siding and window trim

5. Porches
6. Roof
7. Bricks of the chimney
8. Size of the trees
(And more)

If you're not sure what could be told from some of the items, ask your parent for help. There should be at least three or four sentences about each of the items on your list When you're done with your description, your reader should be able to tell, without you saying so, that the house has just been built.

THE OLD HOUSE

Days Three and Four:

In this paper you'll describe the same large house. This time the house is very old, but you'll not tell your reader this. The way you describe the house will give your reader this knowledge. You can again describe the:

1. Lawn
2. Shrubs and flowers
3. Sidewalk
4. Paint on the siding and window trim

5. Porches
6. Roof
7. Bricks of the chimney
8. Size of the trees
(And more)

There should be **at least** four or five sentences about each of the items on your list.

When you're done with your description, your reader should be able to tell that the house is very old and may no longer be lived in.

I recommend you take the next week off from writing.

PROGRESS REPORT

Name:_____ Date:_____

Exercise # 14 **THE NEW HOUSE**

Copy your best sentence for the week on the lines below.

_____

_____

Name one mistake you made this week that you can fix and will avoid next week.

_____

_____

Write the sentence that had this mistake in it.

_____

_____

Write the sentence again showing how you fixed this mistake.

_____

_____

Comments:

#15 THE BALLOON

Skill: CREATION

It should take you at least six days to learn that:
1. Characters have emotions
2. You can create characters who act because of their emotions
3. You can write a very short story with complicated characters in it

PREWRITING

Day One:

Good stories are complicated because every character in them is motivated by feelings, just as we all are motivated by what we feel and think. You'll write a short story in which you'll give your characters emotions.

A scenario is the action line of a play or story. It doesn't have detail, description or dialogue. It's written in present tense. I'll give you the scenario for the story you'll write. Your parent may want to read this scenario with you and point out the actions.

Scenario for "The Balloon"

Betty, an eight-year-old girl, is in the park with her father, whom she sees only on the weekends. He is a kind man but he no longer lives with Betty and her mother. When he visits Betty, he always brings her gifts, and when they are together, he keeps offering to buy her things.

One day, on a walk through the park, he buys her a large, red balloon. There is a small boy, poorly dressed, who has been following the balloon man. He watches Betty's father give the balloon to Betty. He then follows Betty and her father, his eyes on her balloon.

While Betty's father is buying ice cream for them, Betty gives her balloon to the small boy. He runs off with it, a big, happy smile on his face. When Betty's father asks her where her balloon went, Betty looks up to the sky and tells her father that it went where all good balloons want to go.

He smiles at her and tells her he will get her another one. They eat their ice cream and, holding hands, walk on into the park.

66

In order to make this a good story, your reader will have to know what motivates the characters. Motivation is what makes people do things. Your reader, after reading your story, should be able to answer the following questions. Your parent may want to work through the scenario with you and help you think about the questions:

1. Why did Betty's father give Betty so many things?
2. Why did the small boy follow the balloon man and then follow Betty's balloon?
3. Why did Betty give the balloon to the small boy?
4. Why didn't Betty tell her father what she had done with her balloon?
5. Did Betty lie?

Your characters should talk to each other. They should be seen to move. The reader should see them "think" (Ask your parent about this one).

WRITING

Day Two to the End of the Exercise:
I'll start your story for you. You don't have to use this start if you don't want to.

The Balloon

Betty's father held her hand as they entered the park. He was very tall, and when he came on Sundays to visit her and take her out for the day, he always wore a suit. Betty was dressed in her best clothes, so they didn't look much like the others in the park. Most of the people had on comfortable clothes and tennis shoes.

Her tall father looked down at her and said, "What would you like to do today, Betty?" He always asked her that question, and Betty never knew what to say.

You'll have to plan the rest of your story so that your reader will be able to answer that short list of questions at the top of this page.

You should plan on including the following actions and descriptions in your story. Your parent may want to read through this list and talk with you about how you can include the items in your story.

1. Betty will have to see the small boy two or three times and recognize that he wants a balloon.   (Below is an example of how #1 can be included in the story.)

Betty should see the boy early in the story and see that he's looking at the balloons. Later, when her father buys her a balloon, she can see that the boy is looking up at her balloon. She can turn and see him following her and her balloon.

2. Betty and the small boy will have to live in the same "small" world—the world of kids. A world that her father cannot enter (He's too tall and too old).

3. Betty and the boy must be seen to be alike in some ways. They're both small, they're alone (even though she's with her father) and they both want something. The balloon is just a symbol here. (Ask your parent how symbols work or you could check in your library for a dictionary of literary terms.)

4. There must be a reason why the boy doesn't buy his own balloon. This can be indicated by the clothes he wears.

5. The small boy and Betty must exchange "looks." They must talk with their eyes. The boy and Betty must look at each other then at the balloon Betty is holding by its string.

6. Betty must be made to think about the boy before she gives him the balloon. The reader must see her feel for the boy.

7. The reader must understand that Betty doesn't want to lie to her father. She must hesitate before she tells him where the balloon has gone.

8. Betty, while she licks her ice cream cone, could turn and watch the small boy walk off with her balloon.

9. Betty might reach up and hold her father's hand in the same way that she held the string to her balloon.

10. The reader could see Betty, holding her father's hand, going in one direction, and the boy, holding the balloon by the string, going the other way.

Each day for the next five days you'll write more of this story. Your parent each day will read over what you've written. When you've finished the rough draft, take extra time if you need it to write a finished copy. This means that you'll have a chance to check for spelling and punctuation errors.

Your reader should see the park. Don't forget the fountain, the pond with ducks, the other people, the benches where some of them are eating lunch, and the booth where people can buy food, candy and balloons.

I know you didn't ask for advice, but it's free. It's more important for you to do your best work when you're writing than it is to finish on some time schedule. Do the best you can, and if you take longer than I suggest, so what?

I recommend you take the next week off from writing.

PROGRESS REPORT

Name:_____ Date: _____

Exercise # 15 **THE BALLOON**

Copy your best paragraph for the week on the lines below. (Check)

_____

_____

_____

_____

_____

Name one mistake you made this week that you can fix and will avoid next week.

_____

Write the sentence that had this mistake in it.

_____

_____

Write the sentence again showing how you fixed this mistake.

_____

_____

Comments:

#16 WRITING LETTERS

Skill: ORGANIZATION

It may take you six days to learn that you can:
1. Understand the principles of writing business letters
2. Learn where to place the parts of a business letter
3. Write a business letter

PREWRITING

Days One and Two:
This exercise has three parts:
1. A letter of inquiry
2. A letter ordering merchandise
3. A letter of complaint

There are some principles of writing business letters that you should be aware of, and you should use them in this exercise.

Business letters should be:
1. Neat
2. Short
3. Simple
4. Courteous
5. To the point
6. Complete in information

1. **Neat** means that you should type if you can. If this isn't possible, the letter should be written in ink, have no cross-outs, have no dirty marks or smudges, be on unlined paper (but the lines of writing should be even and straight), and have straight margins.

2. **Short** means that you shouldn't say any more in the letter than the reader needs to know. Assume that the reader of the letter is smart and knows his or her job. Explain what you want done or know and let that person get on with the job.

3. **Simple** means that you shouldn't use long sentences if short ones will do. You should use short words and not try to impress the reader with your vocabulary or your ability to write.

4. **Courteous** means that, even if you're mad, you'll be more successful with your letter if you're nice to the person reading it than you'd be if you weren't courteous.

5. **To the point** means that you should tell your reader exactly what information will be needed to give you what you want. Come right out and say it like this: "I want a refund of $3.79 on the defective pen."

6. **Complete in information** means that you should include in your letter all of the facts that the reader will need to know. If the letter were to be about a product that you had bought, you should include:

a) The **name** of the product
b) The **model number**
c) The **price**
d) The **date of purchase**
e) The **store** where it was bought
f) A **description of what was wrong**
g) A list of **what you've done** to get your money back
h) **What you expect** the reader of your letter to do about your problem

WRITING

PART ONE:

You're to write a business letter to a company asking for information about a product or a service. You'll have to make up the names of the company, the product and the address.

You may use one of these suggestions if you can't think of a product:

1. A special tire for your dirt bike from the Tight Grip Co.
2. A replacement for one of the wheels on your skates from the Smooth Ride Co.

Your letter should ask for information on replacement parts and their cost. On the next page is *a very short* model for a business letter. You should copy the format. This means that you should set your letter up with the same placement, spaces and margins.

Of course, your letters will be much more complicated and longer than these examples.

37 Oak Street
Niles, Michigan 49120
June 10, 2001

Non-sag Mattress Co.
2009 Ticking Street
Stripetown, Michigan 49992

Dear Sir:
I would like to replace the "Do not remove" tag on my Non-sag mattress, model number 55585. Please send color selections and prices.

Sincerely,

Bill Smith

PART TWO:

Days Three and Four:
You'll write the same company and ask them to ship you the item you need. You should write in the letter that you're enclosing a check or money order. **This part** of this letter can look like this *short example*:

37 Oak Street
Niles, Michigan 49120
June 15, 2001

Dear Sir:
Please send one white "Do not remove" tag for mattress model number 55585. Enclosed is a money order for $2.00.

Sincerely,

Bill Smith

PART THREE:

Days Five and Six:
In this part of this exercise you're to write the same company and complain that the merchandise you received was not what you had ordered. Remember to include all of the information the company will need to fill your order. Be nice. This letter can look like this **short** example:

---

37 Oak Street
Niles, Michigan 49120
June 23, 2001

Non-sag Mattress Co.
2009 Ticking Street
Stripetown, Michigan 48992

Dear Sir:

On June 12, 2001 I ordered one white "Do not remove" tag for mattress model number 55585. I enclosed a money order for $2.00.
You shipped me a blue tag. Enclosed is the blue tag.
Please send me a white tag.

Sincerely,

Bill Smith

I recommend you take the next week off from writing.

PROGRESS REPORT

Name:_____ Date:_____

Exercise # 16 WRITING LETTERS

Copy your best sentence for the week on the lines below.

_____

_____

Name one mistake you made this week that you can fix and will avoid next week.

_____

_____

Write the sentence that had this mistake in it.

_____

_____

Write the sentence again showing how you fixed this mistake.

_____

_____

Comments:

SPELLING LIST

THE REALLY BIG WRITING PROBLEMS I'VE
SOLVED THIS YEAR

(You might want your parents to help you with this one)

1._____

_____

2._____

_____

3._____

_____

4._____

_____

Why the skills I've learned this year are so important to me: _____

_____

_____

_____

SMALL WRITING PROBLEMS I HAVE SOLVED
THIS YEAR
THAT I'M REALLY PROUD OF

1._____

_____

2._____

_____

3._____

_____

4._____

_____

5._____

_____

6._____

_____

How I feel about this progress I'm making: _____

SECOND SEMESTER REPORT

WRITING SKILLS MASTERY

FIFTH LEVEL WRITING EXERCISES

Student:_____ Date:_____

Parent:_____

Skill   Needs
Mastered Experience

Exercise 9: An Author Makes the Reader Feel
Skill Area: Creation

_____   _____ 1. Understanding that a reader's feelings are controlled
_____   _____ 2. Understanding that these feelings help the reader understand the story
_____   _____ 3. Understanding some techniques authors use
_____   _____ 4. Using reader-control techniques

Exercise 10: Out of Time
Skill Area: Basic

_____   _____ 1. Writing dialogue that follows the story line
_____   _____ 2. Changing tenses in dialogue
_____   _____ 3. Controlling the use of tenses

Exercise 11: My Thumb
Skill Area: Description

_____   _____ 1. Seeing an object as a group of parts
_____   _____ 2. Organizing what is seen
_____   _____ 3. Organizing descriptive writing

Exercise 12: Flashback
Skill Area: Organization

_____   _____ 1. Understanding what a flashback is
_____   _____ 2. Knowing how flashbacks work
_____   _____ 3. Using flashbacks in writing

Exercise 13: Foreshadowing
Skill Area: Organization

_____   _____ 1. Understanding foreshadowing
_____   _____ 2. Knowing how foreshadowing is used
_____   _____ 3. Using foreshadowing in writing

Exercise 14: Old House
Skill Area: Creation

_____   _____ 1. Controlling what the reader understands
_____   _____ 2. Describing an object so that the reader will see it in his mind

Exercise 15: The Balloon
Skill Area: Creation

_____   _____ 1. Understanding that characters have emotions
_____   _____ 2. Creating characters who are motivated by their emotions
_____   _____ 3. Writing a story with complicated characters

Exercise 16: Writing Letters
Skill Area: Organization

_____   _____ 1. Understanding the principles of writing business letters
_____   _____ 2. Learning where to place the parts of business letters
_____   _____ 3. Writing a business letter

EVALUATION OF FIFTH LEVEL WORK

Student Name:_____Date:_____

WRITING PROBLEMS NEEDING FURTHER WORK IN SIXTH LEVEL:

1._____

2._____

3._____

4._____

5._____

6._____

7._____

8._____

9._____

10._____

11._____

12._____

13._____

File this evaluation with your papers to be kept for reference during the sixth level.

COMMON PROBLEMS

with

DEFINITIONS * RULES * EXAMPLES

AMBIGUITY

A statement may be taken in two ways.

1. *She saw the man walking down the street.*

   This can mean either:
   A. *She saw the man when she was walking down the street;* or,
   B. *She saw the man when he was walking down the street.*

2. The use of pronouns *it, she, they, them* that do not have clear antecedents (what they refer to) can create ambiguous sentences:

   Bill looked at the coach when <u>he</u> got the money.

   This can mean either:
   A. *When Bill got the money he looked at the coach;* or,
   B. *Bill looked at him when the coach got the money.*

APOSTROPHE

An apostrophe (') is a mark used to indicate possession or contraction.

Rules:
1. To form the possessive case (who owns it) of a singular noun (one person or thing), add an apostrophe and an *s*.

   Example:

   the girl's coat   Bill's ball   the car's tire

2. To form the possessive case of a plural noun (two or more people or things) ending in *s*, add only the apostrophe.

   Example:

   the boys' car   the cars' headlights

81

3. Do not use an apostrophe for: *his, hers, its, ours, yours, theirs, whose.*

    Example:

    The car was theirs.   The school must teach its students.

4. Indefinite pronouns: (could be anyone) *one, everyone, everybody,* require an apostrophe and an *s* to show possession.

    Example:

    One's car is important.   That must be *somebody's* bat.

5. An apostrophe shows where letters have been omitted in a contraction (making one word out of two).

    Example:

    can't for cannot   *don't* for do not   *it's* for it is
    we've for we have   *doesn't* for does not

    Note that the apostrophe goes in the word where the letter or letters have been left out.

6. Use an apostrophe and an *s* to make the plural of letters, numbers and of words referred to as words.

    Example:

    There are three *b's* and two *m's* in that sentence.
    It was good back in the *1970's.*
    Do not say so many *"and so's"* when you explain things.

AWKWARD WRITING

Awkward writing is rough and clumsy. It can be confusing to the reader and make the meaning unclear. Many times just the changing of the placement of a word or the changing of a word will clear up the awkwardness.

If you read your work out loud or have someone else read to it to you and then to listen to what you're saying, you can catch the awkwardness. Remember that you have to read loud enough to hear your own voice.

1. *Each of you kids will have to bring each day each of the following things: pen, pencil and paper.*

This should be rewritten to read:

Each day bring pens, pencils and paper.

2. *The bird flew down near the ground, and having done this, began looking for bugs or worms because it was easier to see them down low than it had been when it was flying high in the sky.*

There are many problems with that sentence. To get rid of its awkwardness, it could be rewritten to read:

The bird, looking for food, swooped low.

Keep in mind that the point of your writing is for you to give your readers information. The simplest way to do this may be the best way.

CLICHÉ

All of us like to use expressions we have heard or read. Many times you'll use expressions in your writing that you won't realize have been used so many times before that they no longer are fresh and exciting for your readers. The best way to avoid this is to read your work aloud and listen for familiar phrases. Omit them.

round as a dollar	*pretty as a picture*	*tall as a tree*
stopped in his tracks	*stone cold dead*	*fell flat on his face*
snapped back to reality	*graceful as a swan*	*stiff as a board*
limber as a willow	*roared like a lion*	*white as a sheet*

Usually the first expressions young writers think of when they write will be clichés. If you think you've heard of an expression before, don't use it.

COMMAS

You can solve most of your comma problems if you read your work out loud and listen to where your voice drops in each sentence. There is where a comma goes. This will work for about 95% of comma placement. This works because commas are needed and used to make clear the meaning in writing. They indicate a pause or a separation of ideas.

Rules:
1. To separate place names—as in an address, dates, or items in a series
2. To set off introductory or concluding expressions

3. To make clear the parts of a compound sentence
4. To set off transitional or non-restrictive words or expressions in a sentence

Examples:

1. *During the day on May 3, 1989, I began to study.*

I had courses in English, math and geography at a little school in Ann Arbor, Michigan.

The parts of the date should be separated by commas, and the courses in this sentence which come in a list should be separated by commas. You have a choice of whether to put a comma before the *and* just prior to the last item on a list.

2. *After the bad showing on the test, Bill felt he had to study more than he had.*

The introduction—*After the bad showing on the test*—to the central idea of this sentence—*Bill felt he had to study more*—is set off from this central idea by a comma.

3. *Bill went to class to study for the test, and I went to the snack bar to feed the inner beast.*

There are two complete ideas here: 1) *Bill went to study*; and, 2) *I went to eat*. These two ideas can be joined in a compound (two or more things put together) sentence if there's a conjunction (*and*, *but*, *though*) between them and they're separated by a comma.

Notice where the comma is placed in the example below.

4. *Bob, who didn't really care, made only five points on the test.*

The central idea of this fourth sentence is that Bob made only five points on the test. The information given that he didn't care is interesting but not essential to the understanding of the main idea of the sentence. The commas indicate that the words between them are not essential to the meaning of the sentence.

COMMA SPLICE

A comma splice is when the two halves of a compound sentence are joined/separated by a comma.

Example:
Bill had to take the test over again, he felt sorry he would miss the party.

A comma splice can be avoided by writing this sentence in one of the five following ways:

1. *Bill had to take the test over again and felt sorry he would miss the party.*

2. *Bill had to take the test over again; he felt sorry he would miss the party.*

3. *Bill had to take the test over again, and he felt sorry he would miss the party.*

4. *Bill had to take the test over again: he felt sorry he would miss the party.*

5. *Bill had to take the test over again. He felt sorry he would miss the party.*

Notice that the punctuation of each of the above examples gives the reader a different idea about Bill and how he felt.

DIALOGUE STRUCTURE and PUNCTUATION

Dialogue is conversation between two or more people. When shown in writing, it refers to the speech or thoughts of characters.

Rules:

Dialogue can occur either in the body of the writing or on a separate line for each new speaker.

Examples:

1. *John took his test paper from the teacher and said to him, "This looks like we'll get to know each other well." The teacher looked surprised and said with a smile, "I hope so."*

2. *John took his test paper from the teacher and said to him, "This looks like you and I'll get to know each other well."*
The teacher looked surprised and said with a smile, "I hope so."

3. *John took his test paper from the teacher and thought, "This looks like I'll get to know this old man well this year." The teacher looked surprised—almost as if he had read John's mind—and thought, "I hope so."*

FLOWERY WRITING

Some young writers use flowery writing when they want to impress their readers with how many good words they can use to express ideas. This results in the words used becoming more important than the ideas presented.

Rule:

A general rule that should apply is: What you say should be put as simply as possible.

Example:

The red and fiery sun slowly settled into the distant hills like some great, billowing sailing ship sinking beyond the horizon. It cast its pink and violet flags along the tops of the white canvas-clouds where they waved briefly before this ship of light slid beneath the waves of darkness and cast us all, there on the beach, into night.

This is so flowery that it is hard to read without laughing.

It should be rewritten to read:

As the sun set, we remained on the beach, watching the sky darken.

MODIFIER (dangling)

This means that there's nothing for the modifier to modify in the sentence.

Examples:
Getting up, my arms felt tired. (How did the arms get up all by themselves?)

This should read: *When I got up my arms felt tired.*

Coming down the street, my feet wanted to turn into the park. (Again, how did the feet do this?)

This should read: *Coming down the street, I felt as if my feet wanted to turn toward the park.*

Being almost asleep, the accident made me jump. (It's clear the accident could not have been asleep.)

This should read: *I was almost asleep and the accident made me jump.*

OMITTED WORDS

Most of us leave words out of sentences, or leave the endings off of words. You can solve this problem if you read your work out loud and slowly. You must do this slowly enough that you can catch every syllable.

I've had adult students get angry after I have asked them to read what they've written for the fifth or sixth time before they recognized what they had left out.

PARAGRAPH

A paragraph is a sentence or a group of sentences developing one idea or topic.

Rules:
In nonfiction writing, a paragraph consists of a topic sentence which is supported by other sentences giving additional details. A good rule is: A paragraph in this kind of writing should have at least four supportive sentences, making at least five sentences for every paragraph.

Example:

TOPIC SENTENCE: One sentence that introduces the reader to the main idea of the paragraph.

PARAGRAPH DEVELOPMENT: May be made by facts, examples, incidents, comparison, contrast, definition, reasons (in the form of arguments) or by a combination of methods.

PARALLELISM

Parallelism is two or more parts of a single sentence, having equal importance—being structured the same way.

Examples:

1. *We went home to eat and reading*. This should read: *We went home to eat and to read*. This is obvious in such a short sentence, but this is an easy mistake to make when the sentences get complicated.

2. *There are a number of things that a boy must think about when he is planning to take a bike trip. He must think about checking the air pressure in his tires, putting oil on the chain, making sure the batteries in his light are fresh and to make sure his brakes work properly.*

Notice in this list there's a combination of four parallel participles and one infinitive which cannot be parallel in structure. (This sounds like English-teacher talk.)

What it means is the first three items on the list: (1) *checking*, (2) *putting* (3) *making* are parallel, but the fifth item on the list, (5) *to make*, is not structured the same way, and so this last item is not parallel in structure with the first four items.

This sentence should be rewritten to read: *He must think about **checking** the air pressure in his tires, **putting** oil on the chain, **making** sure the batteries in his light are fresh and **making** sure the brakes work properly.*

87

PRONOUN REFERENCE and AGREEMENT

To keep writing from being boring, pronouns are often used instead of nouns.

Rules:
It must be clear to the reader which noun the pronoun is replacing. The pronoun must agree in case, gender and number with that noun. The most common error young writers make is with number agreement.

Examples:

Betty and Janet went to the show, but she didn't think it was so good. (It is not clear which girl didn't like the show.)

If a child comes to dinner without clean hands, they must go back to the sink and wash over. (The word *they* refers to "a child" and the number is mixed.)

This should read: *If children come to dinner without clean hands they should go back and re-wash them.*

Both boys took exams but Bob got a higher score on it. (The pronoun *it* refers to the noun *exams* and the number is mixed here.)

Everybody should go to the show, and they should have their tickets handy. (The problem here is that the word *everybody* is singular and the pronouns *they* and there are plural.) The following words are singular and they need singular verbs: *everybody, anybody, each, someone.*

QUOTATION MARKS

Quotation marks are used to indicate exact words or thoughts and to indicate short works and chapters of long works.

Rule: 1. You should put in quotation marks the direct quotation of a person's words. When you use other marks of punctuation with quotation marks: 1) you should put commas and periods inside the quotation marks; and, 2) put other punctuation marks inside the quotation marks if they're part of the quotation; if they're not part of the quotation, you should put them outside of the quotation marks.

Example: *The salesman said, "This is the gum all the kids are chewing."*

Rule: 2. Put in quotation marks the titles of chapters, articles, other parts of books or magazines, short poems, short stories and songs.

Example: *In this magazine there were two things I really liked: "The Wind Blows Free" and "Flowers," the poems by the young girl.*

REDUNDANCY

Redundancy means using different words to say the same thing. The writer does not gain by this, only confuses and bores the reader.

Examples:

I, myself, feel it is true.
It is plain and clear to see.
Today, in the world, there is not room for lack of care for the ecology.

This is an easy mistake to make, and it'll take conscious thought for you to avoid this problem. There are no exercises that you can do which will help: just use care when you're proofreading your work.

SENTENCE

RUN-ON: This is the combining of two or more sentences as if they were one.

Example:

Bill saw that the fish was too small he put it back in the lake and then put a fresh worm on his hook. (This sentence needs to be broken into two sentences by putting a period between *small* and *he*. It could also be correct with a semicolon between *small* and *he*.)

FRAGMENT: This is part of a sentence which lacks a subject or a verb or both.

Check your sentences to make sure they have both subjects and verbs.

Some writers use fragments effectively. You may do this in your creative writing. Avoid using fragments in your expository papers.

Examples:

Fragments can be powerful if used correctly:

When Janet reached her door, she found it was partly open. A burglar! Someone had been in her house and had left the door open.

SENTENCE VARIETY

Young writers have a tendency to structure all or most of their sentences in the same way. You need to give variety to the structuring of your sentences. A common problem for young writers is that of beginning most sentences with a subject-verb pattern.

Examples:

Janet bought a car. The car was blue. It had a good radio. She liked her car and spent a lot of time in it.

These sentences could be re-written and combined so they all do not start with a subject and verb.

The car Janet bought was blue. Because she liked it so much, she spent a lot of time in it.

SUBJECT-VERB AGREEMENT (number)

Closely related words have matching forms, and, when the forms match, they agree. Subjects and their verbs agree if they both are singular or both are plural.

Rules: Singular subjects require singular verbs, and plural subjects require plural verbs.

Singular: *car, man, that, she, he, it*
Plural: *cars, men, those, women, they*
Singular: *The heater was good.   The heater works well.*
Plural: *The heaters were good.   The heaters work well.*

Most nouns form plurals by adding the letter *s*, as in *bats* and *cats*. The clue is the final *s*.

It is just the opposite with most verbs. A verb ending in *s* is usually singular, as in *puts, yells, is* and *was*.

Most verbs not ending in *s* are plural, as in *they put, they yell*. The exceptions are verbs used with *I* and singular *you*: *I put, you put*.

Most problems come when there's a phrase or clause between the subject and the verb.

Example:

This red car, which is just one of a lot full of cars, is owned by John and Bob. It is easy for some young writers to think that cars is the plural subject and write the sentence this way: *This red car, which is just one of a whole lot of cars, are owned by John and Bob.*

The subject of this sentence *This red car* is singular; there are just a lot of words between the subject and the verb, and it confuses the number.

TENSE ERROR

Tense errors occur when writers mix past and present tenses and do not have justification for changing from one to the other.

Rules.
1. Present tense is used to describe actions that are taking place at the time of the telling of the event.

    Example: *John is in the house. Mr. Jones lives there.*

2. Past tense is used to describe actions that have already happened.

    Example: *John was in the house. Mr. Jones lived there.*

3. Future tense is used to describe actions that will happen.

    Example: *John will be in the house. Mr. Jones will live there.*

National Writing Institute Order Form

	Qty.	Total

☐ **Writing Strands 1**
Oral work for ages 3-8 $14.95 ea. ____ _____

☐ **Writing Strands 2**
About 7 years old $18.95 ea. ____ _____

☐ **Writing Strands 3**
Starting program ages 8-12 $18.95 ea. ____ _____

☐ **Writing Strands 4**
Any age after Level 3 or starting
program at age 13 or 14 $18.95 ea. ____ _____

☐ **Writing Strands 5**
Any age after Level 4 or starting
program at age 15 or 16 $20.95 ea. ____ _____

☐ **Writing Strands 6**
17 or any age after Level 5 $20.95 ea. ____ _____

☐ **Writing Strands 7**
18 or any age after Level 6 $22.95 ea. ____ _____

☐ **Writing Exposition**
Senior high school and
after Level 7 $22.95 ea. ____ _____

☐ **Creating Fiction**
Senior high school and
after Level 7 $22.95 ea. ____ _____

☐ *Evaluating Writing*
Parents' manual for all levels
of *Writing Strands* $19.95 ea. ____ _____

☐ **Reading Strands**
Parents' manual for story and
book interpretation, all grades $22.95 ea. ____ _____

☐ **Communication and Interpersonal Relationships**
Communication manners
(teens) $17.95 ea. ____ _____

☐ **Dragonslaying Is for Dreamers - package**
1st novel in *Dragonslaying* trilogy
(early teens) and parent's manual
for analyzing the novel. $18.95 ea. ____ _____

☐ **Dragonslaying Is for Dreamers - novel only**
          $9.95 ea. ____ _____

☐ **Dragonslaying Is for Dreamers - audio book**
          $25.00 ea. ____ _____

☐ **Axel Meets the Blue Men**
2nd novel in *Dragonslaying*
trilogy (teens) $9.95 ea. ____ _____

☐ **Axel's Challenge**
Final novel in *Dragonslaying*
trilogy (teens) $9.95 ea. ____ _____

☐ *Dragonslaying Trilogy*
All three novels in series $25.00 set ____ _____

☐ **Dragonslaying Trilogy + Parents' Manual**
Three novels plus parents' manual for first novel
          $32.99 set ____ _____

SUBTOTAL: _____

Texas residents add **7.25%** sales tax .... _____

U.S. Shipping:
$2.00 per book (**$5.00 Minimum**) .... _____

Outside U.S. Shipping:
$4.00 per book (**$12.00 Minimum**) .... _____

TOTAL U.S. FUNDS .... _____

☐ VISA ☐ DISCOVER ☐ MasterCard

Account Number

☐☐☐☐ — ☐☐☐☐ — ☐☐☐☐ — ☐☐☐☐ — ☐☐

Expiration date: Month ☐☐   Year ☐☐

_____
Signature

(PLEASE PRINT) We ship U.P.S. to the 48 states, so please no P.O. #.

Name: _____

Street: _____

City: _____

State: _____ Zip: _____

Phone: (_____) _____

E-Mail: _____

SHIPPING INFORMATION
Continental US : We ship via UPS ground service. Most customers will receive their orders within 10 business days.

Alaska, Hawaii, US Military addresses and US territories: We ship via US Priority Mail. Orders generally arrive within 2 weeks.

Outside U. S.: We generally ship via Air Mail. Delivery times vary.

RETURNS
Our books are guaranteed to please you. If they do not, return them within 30 days and we'll refund the full purchase price.

PRIVACY
We respect your privacy. We will not sell, rent or trade your personal information.

Prices valid through 03/31/03.

INQUIRIES AND ORDERS:
Phone: (800) 688-5375
Fax: (888) 663-7855 TOLLFREE
Write: **National Writing Institute**
          624 W. University #248
          Denton, TX 76201-1889
E-mail: info@writingstrands.com
Homepage: www.writingstrands.com